Annie Sloan's
DECORATIVE
PAINT EFFECTS
A Step-by-Step Course

Annie Sloan's
DECORATIVE
PAINT EFFECTS
A Step-by-Step Course

Photography by Geoff Dann

COLLINS & BROWN

First published in Great Britain in 1996
by Collins & Brown Limited
London House
Great Eastern Wharf
Parkgate Road
London SW11 4NQ

5 7 9 8 6

British Library Cataloguing-in-Publication Data:
A catalogue record for this book
is available from the British Library.

ISBN 1 85585 2470 (hardback edition)

ISBN 1 85585 2950 (paperback edition)

Conceived, edited and designed by
Collins & Brown Limited

Editor Colin Ziegler
Editorial Assistant Claire Waite
Art Director Roger Bristow
Designer Steve Wooster
DTP Designer Claire Graham
Photographer Geoff Dann

Reproduction by Master Image, Singapore

Printed and Bound in Portugal

Contents

Introduction

THE FASCINATING CHARACTERISTIC of the paint techniques shown in this book is that so many effects and variations can be achieved using the same basic materials. The secret ingredient for all the effects is the glaze: a slow-drying, transparent medium that serves as the carrier for the color, whether paint or dry powder pigment. Unlike paint, which dries relatively quickly, glaze dries slowly, allowing you to continue working on

Ragging
Ragging (see pp. 22–25) is an adaptable technique that produces an irregular effect. Dab a cotton rag firmly onto wet glaze to reveal the base color in places. The effect is delicate when similar colors are used, and more lively when the contrast between the two – here, terra-cotta on warm yellow – is pronounced.

Sponging
Sponging (see pp. 26–29) is quick and easy to do and produces a regular, dappled effect. You can either sponge on your second color as here – a dark gray has been sponged onto a pale gray basecoat – or you can brush on the second color and then use a sponge to remove it in places.

Colorwashing
Colorwashing (see pp. 30–37) gives a carefree, natural look. By wiping gently over wet glaze with a soft cloth, you remove the brushmarks and give it a loose feel that works particularly well on walls. Choose colors quite close in tone and use the darker one on top – here, warm yellow ocher on off-white.

a wet surface to produce a decorative finish. Using special brushes, sponges and combs or just everyday materials like rags and newspaper you can create attractive patterns combining base color and glaze color. Since it is transparent, the glaze gives an extra dimension to the paint beneath which remains more or less visible depending on the technique.

Although paint effects may look complicated, they are in fact very easy to do. All the techniques in this book have been carried out with water-base glazes, which are simpler to use than oil glazes especially for the beginner. You can experiment with different mixes: more or less glaze with more or less color to give different degrees of opacity.

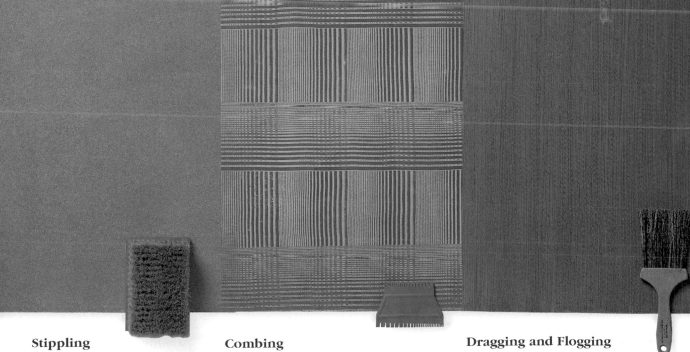

Stippling
Stippling (see pp. 38–43) provides a very sophisticated, even effect, that, from a distance, can look untextured. It is at its most subtle when a lighter basecoat – here, pale blue – is covered by a darker shade of the same color.

Combing
Combing (see pp. 44–49) creates a strong dramatic finish, since the comb concentrates the top color into lines, allowing the base color to show through clearly. This is most obvious when dark and light colors – here, pale blue on dark red – are used in combination.

Dragging and Flogging
Dragging and flogging (see pp. 50–57) are developed from woodgraining techniques and, by using long, coarse-bristled brushes, produce a variegated, striped look. Flogging (top) gives a more subtle look than dragging (above), but with both the stripes are clearer the greater the color contrast between the basecoat and the glaze.

Each technique has its own individual character. Some, like stippling (see pp. 38–43) and dragging (see pp. 50–55), lend themselves well to formal situations, particularly when done in traditional colors such as beige or olive green. But in different color combinations, such as terra-cotta over bright yellow with blue dragged horizontally to make a checkered pattern, the look is anything but formal. You get the most dramatic results when you use strongly contrasting colors, while colors close to each other in tone produce a more restrained, conventional look, especially when the glaze color is darker than the color beneath. For greater depth of color you can add a third or even a fourth layer in the same or a different color. And, for added interest, you can

Patterning with Cloth

The soft, cloudy look is achieved by using cheesecloth/mutton cloth, a finely knitted cotton fabric (see pp. 58–61). A piece of the fabric is formed into a small pad and dabbed over the wet glaze. The fabric print leaves a deliberately uneven texture.

Rag Rolling

This effect (see pp. 62–65) uses two techniques: first the glaze is stippled, then, while it is still wet, a crumpled rag is rolled over the surface, removing some of the glaze to reveal the color beneath.

Frottage

Frottage (see pp. 66–71) is a French word meaning "rubbing". This is the only technique that does not use glaze. It is done using thinned-down paint over which an absorbent material such as newspaper or fabric is rubbed. Each new "rubbing" produces a different effect making a random pattern.

even use different techniques next to each other on the same surface, or even on top of each other.

The most important thing to remember is that you can't go wrong: if you don't like what you have just done, wipe it off and start again. So feel free to experiment and don't worry! Paint effects are great fun to do and very rewarding when you see a room or piece of furniture transformed by your efforts from something commonplace into something unique.

Happy painting!

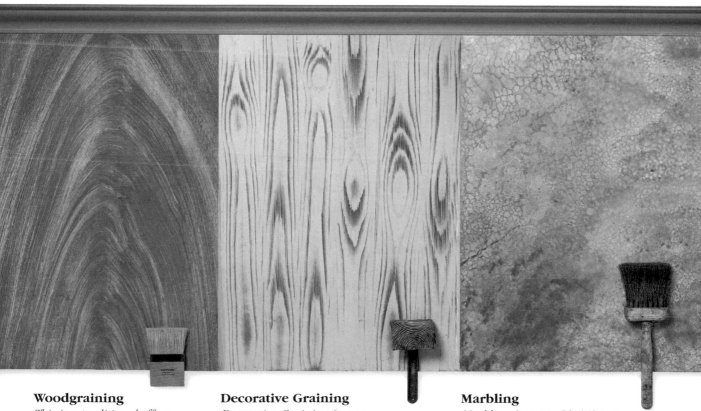

Woodgraining
This is a traditional effect in which paint and glaze are used to imitate wood (see pp. 72–77). Techniques are shown for oak, mahogany, and maple graining – these can be adapted to reproduce other woods. Careful observation and accuracy are needed for successful results.

Decorative Graining
Decorative Graining (see pp. 78–81) is a quick form of woodgraining, using a special tool to make lots of decorative effects, from obviously fake folk woodgraining to producing a finish like moiré or watered silk. Accurate imitation of wood is not the aim.

Marbling
Marbling (see pp. 82–91) is a very old technique and uses a combination of other basic techniques such as sponging and ragging. A badger-hair brush is the essential tool, used to soften the glaze and give it the appearance of smooth marble.

Preparing Surfaces

ANY SURFACE THAT CAN BE painted on can be given a special paint effect. The only constraint is that the surface should be a little porous and not too shiny. Glass and ceramics are difficult to paint on but speciality products are available for this purpose. Rough wall surfaces – even brick, stone, unplaned wood, and textured wallpaper – can all be treated, provided an appropriate technique is chosen. However, a smooth surface offers the greatest choice of techniques and the best chance for a successful result. It is worth taking the time, therefore, to fill cracks in walls and strip and sand furniture carefully before painting.

Stripping Furniture

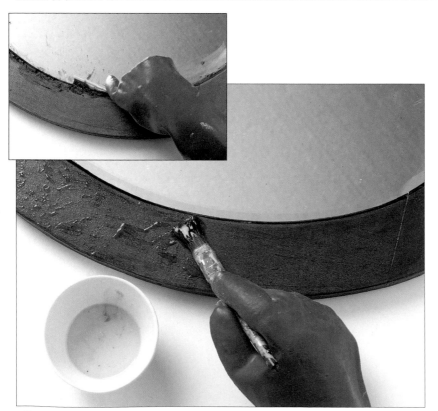

2 Remove the softened paint or varnish with coarse and then fine steelwool.

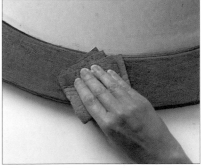

1 Old paint and varnish must be removed before painting furniture. Wearing rubber gloves, apply chemical stripper over the surface with a paintbrush. Use an old toothbrush to get into the crevices of carved or molded surfaces (inset). Leave the stripper on until the old coat has bubbled up.

3 Wipe off excess stripper with an absorbent cloth and the neutralizer recommended by your product. If you are applying water-base varnish, do not use turpentine or white spirit.

Filling Cracks

1 Using a sharp pointed tool such as a screwdriver, dig out the loose plaster from the crack.

2 Using a trowel, lay a generous amount of filler over the crack. Cover about 18in/45cm at a time.

3 With the flat edge of the trowel, work the filler into the crack, pulling the trowel down to make a smooth surface.

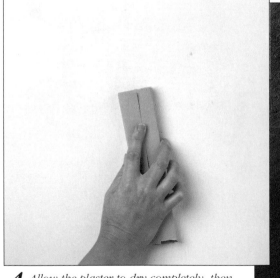

4 Allow the plaster to dry completely, then rub over the surface with fine-grade sandpaper wrapped around a block of wood (above). Once you have brushed off the dust left by sanding, apply the basecoat in preparation for the glaze (right). If the surface is still not smooth enough, sand it once again and apply another basecoat.

Basic Equipment

THE BASIC TOOLS YOU NEED for glazing are the same as for any painting job: drop cloths/dust sheets for protecting floors and furniture, rags for wiping up spills, and rollers and brushes of different sizes for applying the basecoat and glaze. (Speciality brushes are recommended for individual techniques; these are shown on the relevant pages.) For typical painting tasks, the paint you buy is ready-mixed. When glazing, it can be useful to have an assortment of bowls and basins for mixing and experimenting with different colors.

Applying the Basecoat

Rollers allow you to apply paint quickly over a large flat area, but they leave a fine "orange peel" texture which you may not want for the final basecoat. For the best results apply the final coat with a brush. Stippling and patterning with cloth, in particular, need a very smooth, even surface. Special brushes are not required, just use one that feels comfortable.

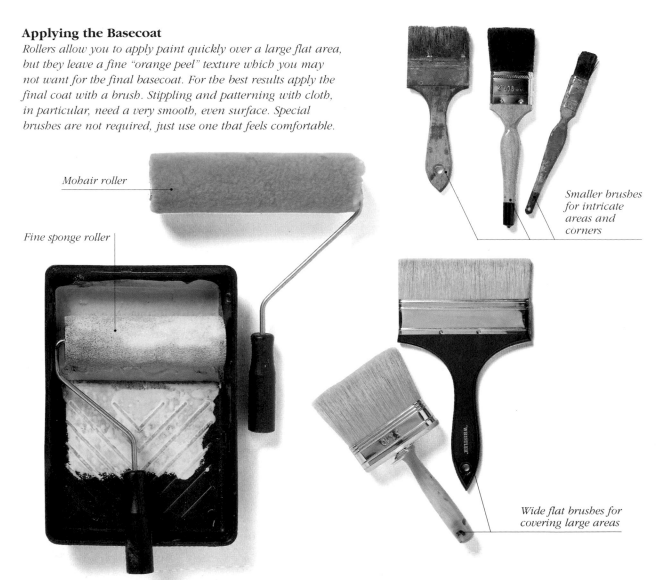

Mohair roller

Fine sponge roller

Smaller brushes for intricate areas and corners

Wide flat brushes for covering large areas

Applying Glaze

Use flat-ended brushes for applying oil-base glaze and oval-shaped for applying water-base glaze. Several widths of brush may be needed, depending on the size of the surface being covered.

Oval-shaped brushes for applying water-base glaze

Artist's fitch for painting intricate areas

Flat-ended brushes for applying oil-base glaze

Other Equipment

You will need extra equipment for preparing your glazes and keeping surfaces clean. A plastic bucket or bowl is useful for mixing glazes and glaze colors, and a glass jar is ideal for mixing oil glaze and pigment to the proper consistency. Use a drop cloth or dust sheet to protect the surfaces you do not want paint or glaze to spill on, and a piece of cloth is useful for wiping surfaces clean and removing excess glaze.

Plastic paint bucket for mixing glaze

Thin brush for mixing and painting

Bowl for mixing glaze colors

Rags for wiping up spills

Glass jar

Drop cloth/dust sheet

Types of Glaze

Most paint effects are achieved with a glaze, which is a translucent medium that can be colored with paint or pigment. Colored glaze is applied to the surface and then manipulated into patterns with cloths, brushes, and sponges, revealing in places the color of the basecoat underneath. Both water- and oil-base glazes are now available. Oil-base glazes (see opposite) were used traditionally and are still preferred by some professional painters and decorators since they can give greater depth of color. However, they are now being superseded by water-base glazes, which are easy to use and more environmentally friendly. In this book we use water-base glazes, although the technique is similar whichever glaze you use.

Normal Water-base Glaze

Use this type of glaze for all the decorative paint techniques in this book except for woodgraining and marbling (see below). To color it simply add water-base paint. On a satin-finish basecoat it will produce a crisp look and on a flat basecoat the effect will be dry and chalky. It is easier to use it over a middle-sheen finish since the glaze will quickly soak into a flat basecoat, giving you less time to work.

Water-base Glaze for Use with Universal Stainers and Pigments

Use this type of glaze for woodgraining and marbling since it creates a very transparent look that both techniques require. Color the glaze by adding universal stainers or pigment – add a little at a time, until you have the required degree of opacity. This type of glaze dries quite quickly so apply it to small areas at a time.

Water-base paint

Normal water-base glaze

Water-base glaze for woodgraining and marbling

Dry powder pigment

Universal stainers or colorizers

Store-bought Oil-base Glazes

Oil-base glaze can be bought either in a transparent form or as "scumble" glaze which is pre-colored in wood colors. It is made with plant-based substances such as linseed oil and turpentine. To use the clear glaze you mix one part oil-base glaze with one part turpentine, and then color with pigments or oil-base paint. You should use them over a middle-sheen or eggshell basecoat.

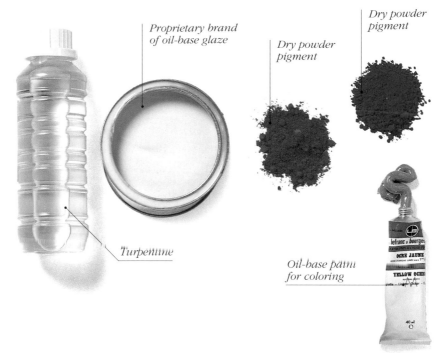

Proprietary brand of oil-base glaze

Dry powder pigment

Dry powder pigment

Turpentine

Oil-base paint for coloring

Homemade Oil-base Glazes

Everyone has their own recipe but you basically mix "boiled linseed oil", turpentine, and a dryer (to accelerate the drying time) in roughly equal proportions and then color with pigment or oil paint. They are usually used over oil-base paints, but some water-base paints are also suitable.

Dry powder pigment

Oil-base paint

Dryer

Turpentine

Boiled linseed oil

Using Glazes

T HE AMOUNT OF PAINT or coloring agent that you mix in with your glaze depends on how opaque you want your glaze to be. The more paint you add the more opaque the effect will be. With normal water-base glaze (see p. 14) you should mix four to six parts glaze to one part paint. Remember that the more paint there is, the quicker it dries, leaving less time to complete your effect.

Your prime concern is that the glaze does not dry out before you complete your effect. If glazing a large area therefore, apply the glaze in sections for certain techniques and in strips for others.

Levels of Opacity
Glaze can have either a lot or a little paint mixed with it. The more paint is added the more opaque the effect. Here, a green glaze was applied over a blue ragged background. On the left it was simply painted on, while on the right it was also ragged. The progression from top to bottom shows that when more and more paint is added, the background blue is obliterated.

Painting in Sections

1 For ragging, sponging, stippling, colorwashing, patterning with cloth, and some combing techniques, apply the glaze over an area about 18 in/45 cm square.

2 Carry out the required technique on the glaze, leave an unworked strip on one side, known as the wet edge. Paint the next area of glaze right into this so that a line is not created where the two sections meet.

Painting in Strips

1 For dragging, flogging, and some combing techniques, apply the glaze in a strip from ceiling to molding. Drag, flog, or comb down, leaving a wet edge so the next strip can be joined invisibly. Wipe off any glaze that has spread onto the molding.

2 Drag or flog from the bottom of the wall by drawing the brush upward. This helps to break up the brushmarks and to avoid a build-up of glaze at the edge.

GLAZING ON RAISED SURFACES

Paint effects also work well on rough or irregular surfaces such as raised wallpaper. You can either choose a technique to mask the texture or to accentuate it. As a general rule choose an effect that produces an irregular, highly patterned surface, such as ragging, to disguise a pattern and a plain, smooth effect, such as colorwashing, to enhance it. However this does depend on the pattern you are glazing over. You can see how the pattern on the wallpaper below is far more noticeable after it has been dragged as opposed to stippled, since the basecoat shows through, emphasizing the pattern on the dragging.

Dragging

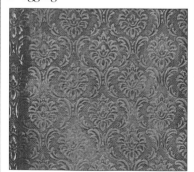

Stippling

Varnishes and Waxes

THERE ARE TWO REASONS FOR varnishing or waxing over a paint effect: for protection and for decorative effect. Glazed paint effects are relatively durable, but they need a protective coating if used on an object or area that gets hard wear. Wax does offer some protection but varnish is best for areas that need to be wiped over frequently, such as tabletops, kitchen, or bathroom cupboards or walls, that may get marked or scraped. Dark colors often look good with gloss varnish, while mellow, earthy colors are better enhanced by wax or matt varnish.

Satin (semigloss) Varnish

Both the paint sample and molding are covered with a coat of water-base, also known as acrylic, varnish. The varnish is quick-drying and has a glossy finish. You could create the same effect with an oil-base glossy varnish. The latter takes longer to dry but gives the surface a slight yellow tinge that emphasises and deepens the colors.

Varnish brush

Satin water-base varnish

Flat Varnish

Water-base flat varnish protects the surface without making it greaseproof. For stronger protection with a flat finish first coat your surface with a satin varnish, and then with a flat varnish. Completely flat oil-base varnishes are difficult to obtain. Here, the paint sample and molding were coated with a flat water-base varnish tinted with a green pigment. Pigment can be added to all varnishes or you can buy colored varnishes ready-made.

Varnish brush

Colored flat water-base varnish

APPLYING VARNISH AND WAX

You should apply varnish in a thin, even layer using a flat brush. Brush it out with the tip of the brush.

Apply wax with very soft, fine-grade steelwool. Leave it for 10 to 15 minutes so the wax penetrates the surface and then buff it with a soft cloth.

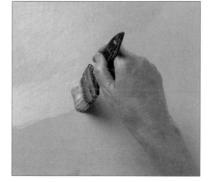

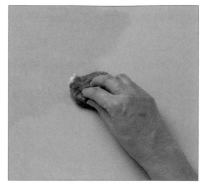

Applying varnish

Applying wax

Clear Wax

This offers some protection to the surface, but not as much as varnish. It imparts a soft, attractive sheen far from the deaden-ing finish of flat varnish but less shiny than gloss or satin varnish. You must use a wax which does not contain Toluene since this is a paint stripper.

Clear wax

Fine steelwool

Cotton cloth

Dark Wax

You can use a dark-colored wax to create an aged or antiqued look. Here, dark-colored wax was used to darken the colors on both the paint sample and the molding. On the latter it was allowed to settle more thickly in the crevices, simulating grime accumu-lated over the years.

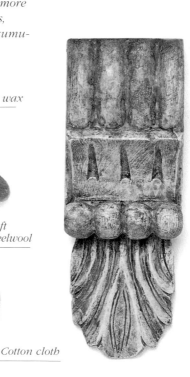

Dark wax

Soft steelwool

Cotton cloth

Techniques

RAGGING

SPONGING

COLORWASHING

STIPPLING

COMBING

DRAGGING & FLOGGING

PATTERNING WITH CLOTH

RAG ROLLING

FROTTAGE

WOODGRAINING

DECORATIVE GRAINING

MARBLING

COMBINING TECHNIQUES

Ragging

Ragged Wall

A yellow ocher glaze, darkened with a hint of terra-cotta red, was ragged over an off-white background. When choosing the color combinations for your wall, avoid highly contrasting colors unless you want a very dramatic effect.

RAGGING PRODUCES a lively irregular pattern that is suitable for decorating both walls and pieces of furniture. You bunch a rag the size of a large napkin in your hand and then dab it firmly onto the wet glaze, so that it removes the glaze in parts, revealing the base color underneath. A soft cotton rag is most commonly used, but different materials make different patterns depending on their thickness and absorbency – heavy linen, for instance, makes a bold crisp effect, while polyester cloth gives a lighter, more undefined look.

The color of the basecoat is vital in ragging because so much of it is revealed. The standard style is to cover it with a glaze a few tones darker – the more similar the colors are, the subtler the effect.

TOOLS & MATERIALS

Paintbrush

Stippling brush for corners

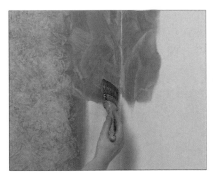

Cotton rag

Glaze colored with water-base paints

The Basic Technique

1 Apply a liberal coat of glaze over a maximum area of 20in/130cm square, using criss-cross brushstrokes.

2 Dab a bunched-up rag over the wet glaze to lift it off. Leave a strip unragged along the edges.

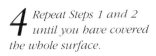

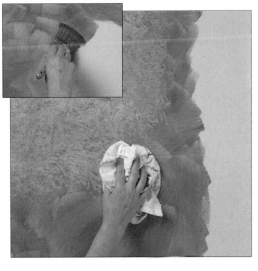

3 After about 10 dabs, re-form the rag so it doesn't become saturated. When the whole rag is sodden, replace it with a new one.

4 Repeat Steps 1 and 2 until you have covered the whole surface.

Avoiding Glaze Build-up in Corners

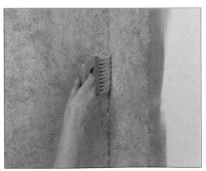

1 Apply glaze to the surface in the same way as in The Basic Technique, *but be careful so it's not too thick in the corner.*

2 Dab the rag gently into the corner, applying more pressure to one side than the other to prevent the glaze from being smeared.

3 When the glaze is nearly dry – after about half an hour – dab firmly into the corner with a stippling brush to remove any excess glaze.

Special Effects

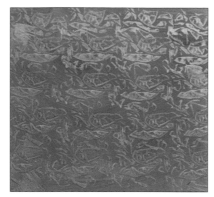

It is usual to rag until the brushmarks are no longer visible. But you can make a special feature of them by leaving parts of the surface unragged.

Over small areas, such as panels, you can make a pattern by dabbing at regular intervals while keeping the rag in the same position in your hand.

Double Ragging

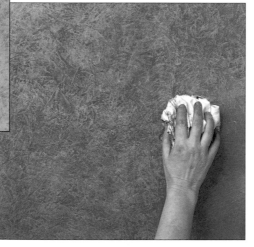

When the glaze is dry, you layer in a different color, or a deeper shade of the same color, to intensify the effect. This also lets you adjust a color that is not quite right.

PITFALLS

A layer of glaze that is too thick results in a glutinous and bubbly surface (below). A layer of glaze that is spread too far or made with only a little paint will make a weak effect when ragged (bottom).

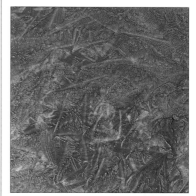

Glaze too thick

Glaze too thin

Ragged Frame

LEFT This frame was covered with a coat of cool gray-blue and then ragged over with a warm chocolate-brown glaze.

Double-Ragged Box
BELOW The yellow ocher basecoat on this box was ragged over twice in a dark red to give a greater intensity of color.

Ragged Candlestick
LEFT The dark, subtle effect on this candlestick was achieved by ragging a rich, clear blue over a brown basecoat.

COLOR COMBINATIONS

Dark red on light gray

Dark green on paler green

Yellow ocher on terra-cotta red

Dark blue on off-white

RAGGING WITH OTHER MATERIALS

Plastic wrap and other types of plastic give a strong, clearly defined pattern that works well on furniture. If you use it on walls, keep the colors close in tone to stop the effect from being overwhelming. Paper towel works well on all surfaces. It gives a soft, slightly spotted finish.

Plastic wrap

Paper towel

Using plastic wrap

Using paper towel

Sponging

Sponged Tabletop

The deep, rich color of this tabletop was achieved by sponging several shades of turquoise together with a little brighter green for contrast over a black basecoat. Layers were built up for a dense effect.

SPONGING PRODUCES a lively, informal effect that can be achieved in two different ways. Both are quick and easy to do. You can apply colored glaze with a brush over the basecoat – which can be either darker or lighter in tone – and then partially remove it with a sponge. This is called "sponging off". Or, the glaze can be applied directly with a sponge, called "sponging on". A natural sea sponge gives good results by making small, irregular spots of color. Sponging off creates a denser effect, while sponging on gives a lighter look. Responging with other colors gives greater depth.

Sponging on can be done just using paint without mixing in a glaze, especially on small areas, but the use of glaze helps to build up translucent layers of color, adding to the impression of depth.

TOOLS & MATERIALS

Brush for
applying glaze

Large
sponge

Small sponge
for sponging
in corners

Blue glaze

The Basic Technique

1 *Generously paint on the colored glaze. The brushstrokes can be uneven, but the background surface should be well covered.*

2 *With a damp sponge, dab all over the glaze, pressing firmly to disguise any brushstrokes. Change the angle of your wrist to avoid a regular pattern. Leave a wet edge.*

3 *Again using a brush, work into the wet edge, applying a generous amount of glaze for the next section.*

4 *Continue as before, sponging over the brushstrokes. Rinse the sponge in a bucket of water when it has absorbed a lot of glaze, squeezing out well.*

Sponging a Corner

1 *Brush the glaze on both walls and into the corner, working it well in. Dab off the glaze from the walls as explained in The Basic Technique.*

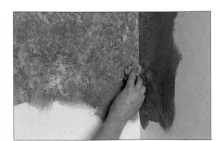

2 *In order to dab right into the corner, use a small sponge or break off a piece of the large sponge.*

Double Sponging

You can achieve interesting effects by building up layers of different colors. Dab on colors next to each other or overlap them to produce a third color. Sponging on and sponging off can also be mixed. Sponging off often gives a more solid base, over which you can sponge on other colors or tones to create depth and highlights. Or, sponge on several colors to give a subtly flecked effect.

1 Use two, three, four, or more colors to build up density. Here, the first color is applied lightly, letting the background show through.

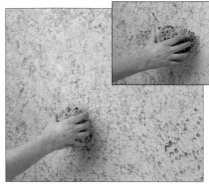

2 The second and third layers of glaze, in dark red and pale yellow, are applied. The previous layer may be slightly wet, but if you make a mistake you will have to start again.

3 The final layer, dark blue-gray glaze, is applied. Painting on a layer of varnish between layers protects previous work if you have to wipe off or reapply glaze.

Using Synthetic Sponges

Using rectangular synthetic sponges gives a very different result from natural sponges. Here, a deliberately hard-edged effect is created using different sized sponges with two colors of glaze.

PITFALLS

Sponging on is less successful if the glaze color contrasts too much with the color of the basecoat (below left). Also, if the sponging is too far apart – leaving large gaps – the effect is patchy. Sponging off looks heavy and coarse if the glaze is too thick and dark (below right*).*

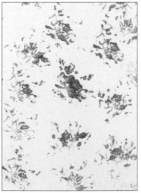

Too much contrast and too far apart

Glaze too thick

COLOR COMBINATIONS

Dark green, then khaki, on pale olive green

Black on bright blue

Yellow ocher on deep red

Deep red on bright green

Sponged Wall

ABOVE A pink-toned terracotta glaze was applied with a brush over an off-white basecoat. The glaze was then sponged off to produce an evenly dappled effect.

Sponged Candlestick

RIGHT The stone effect on this candlestick was achieved by sponging on shades of ocher, gray, and dark cream irregularly over a cream base.

Striped Wall

ABOVE Blue and white stripes were painted on the wall with a roller. Pale blue was sponged over the blue and a darker blue over the white.

Sponged Chair

ABOVE The chair was first painted blue then reds and yellows were sponged on the seat and back slats.

Colorwashing

THIS TECHNIQUE RESULTS in different characteristics depending on the colors you use. With earthy ochers the effect is reminiscent of an old lime-washed wall with contrasting dark and faded patches. With strong, rich colors, such as crimson or emerald green, the result is like oriental lacquer, especially when enhanced with a coat of gloss or satin varnish. Soft pastel colors look best either left natural or with a coat of flat varnish (see pp. 18–19). Unlike other paint techniques, which are carried out in strips or patches, you can cover a large surface area with glaze at a time because, when colorwashing, you only wipe or brush off the glaze when it is nearly dry to avoid leaving scratch marks. If the glaze dries out too much you can use a lightly dampened cloth.

Colorwashed Fireplace

The simple shape of this fireplace was given interest by subtle colorwashing. Over a basecoat of pale blue-gray, glazes of blue, mahogany red, and a dark mixture of the two were applied in patches of varying intensity. The glazes were lightly wiped over, allowed to dry, then reapplied to strengthen the depth of color. The sides of the mantel shelf and edges of the side panels were wiped off with a soft cloth while the glaze was still wet to create a contrasting border.

COLORWASHING IN CLOSE-UP

This detail shows the contrast between the colorwashed effect built up in several layers and the paler edges where the top layers of glaze have been wiped off.

TOOLS & MATERIALS

Paintbrush for applying glaze

Smaller brush for corners and edges

Cheesecloth/ mutton cloth

Mixed glaze

The Basic Technique

1 Paint the glaze over the whole area to be covered and allow it to dry until it can be worked on without scratching the glaze. If the area is too large the glaze may dry too quickly, in which case work in patches, leaving a wet edge to work into.

2 Wipe over the wall with a soft cloth, using strokes of different lengths in all directions. Press hard enough to expose the basecoat but not to remove all the glaze.

3 The cloth will become saturated with glaze as you work, so refold it and begin wiping again with a fresh section of cloth.

4 Continue smoothing out the glaze with the cloth until all the brushmarks are hidden and the color is evenly spread.

Colorwashing Above a Dado Rail

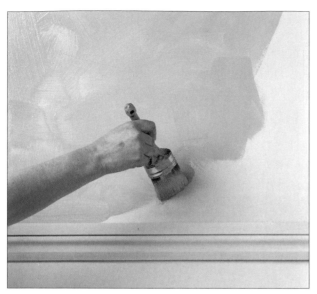

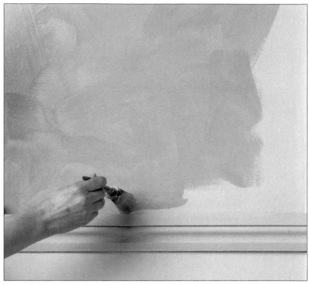

1 *Using a 3 in/75 mm paintbrush, apply a generous layer of glaze to the area of the wall above the dado rail, taking care not to come too close to the dado rail itself.*

2 *Using a smaller brush (here, 1½in/38mm), apply the glaze carefully right up to the edge of the rail. Do not overload the brush.*

4 *Using a small cloth pad, wipe off any excess glaze in the recess between rail and wall.*

3 *When the glaze is almost dry, wipe it off in all directions using a soft cloth (see* The Basic Technique, *p. 31, steps 2–4).*

Double Colorwashing

A second layer of glaze in a different color, or in different shade of the first color, can be applied to intensify, deepen or lighten the first layer. The bigger the contrast between the two colors you

choose, the more distinct the effect, since when the second glaze layer is wiped off, the background color will show through. To alter the look further, you can then apply more layers if desired.

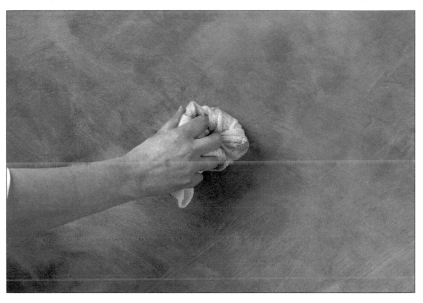

1 Brush on the second layer of glaze (here, reddish brown) when the first layer (here, pale yellow ocher) is dry (see The Basic Technique, *p. 31).*

2 When the surface is nearly dry, wipe over it with a soft rag, removing some of the second layer and allowing the first color to show through.

Colorwashing a Cornice

1 This technique suits any carved or molded surface. Using a color a few tones darker than the basecoat, paint the glaze on with a small brush, working it well into the crevices.

2 When the glaze is nearly dry, wipe gently over the molded surface with a soft cloth. You may need to apply more pressure in certain areas to get an even look.

Colorwashing a Carved Object

Colorwashing can be used to emphasize the depth of carving and molding. The darker colored glaze or paint accumulates in the crevices but is wiped off the raised areas, which, being lighter, then appear more prominent. This technique gives a pleasantly "aged" look to a new object such as the plaque shown here, as the darker color resembles dirt that has built up in the crevices over the years.

1 *For a denser effect use paint rather than glaze. Having painted on the basecoat (here, deep terra-cotta) and varnished it (see pp. 18–19) to prevent the second coat from being absorbed by the plaster of the plaque, paint on the second coat (here, brown-black).*

2 *When the paint is nearly dry, gently wipe a soft cloth over the face, using more pressure on the raised surfaces to remove more of the darker paint and so highlight the molding.*

3 *If the paint has dried or more needs to be removed, wipe over the raised areas with a lightly dampened cloth.*

The Finished Plaque

RIGHT The contrast between the lighter and darker areas on the finished plaque gives a convincing antique effect.

Using More than Two Colors

1 *You can apply more than two colors side by side, rather than overlaying them as in double colorwashing. First paint on patches of glaze (here, green), leaving spaces for the next color.*

2 *Cover all the empty areas with another layer of glaze in a color of similar intensity (here, light blue). To give strength and contrast, also dab on small patches of paint in a third color (here, dark blue).*

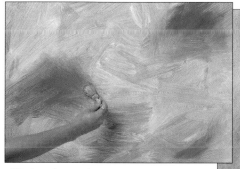

3 *Brush out the paint thoroughly to merge the darker color into the glaze. The colors should flow into each other, without any harsh edges.*

4 *Wipe all over the surface with a soft cloth in a circular polishing motion, smoothing out the colors. The result should be a soft, cloudy effect.*

COLORWASHING WITH BRUSHES

You can use brushes instead of a cloth to wipe off the glaze; this gives a coarser effect, showing the marks of the bristles. For a softer look, hold the tip of the brush at right angles to the surface and wipe gently as with a cloth. A soft wallpaper brush leaves less distinct lines than a hard brush.

Wallpapering brush

House painter's brush

Colorwashing with a hard brush

Colorwashing with a soft brush

Colorwashed Door

RIGHT The bright orange basecoat on the door frame was colorwashed with rich brown glaze. On the panels, the green basecoat was covered with deep blue glaze, which was wiped off in places to make tree shapes and other patterns.

Blue over Green

ABOVE The peppermint green basecoat was colorwashed with sage green glaze. When dry, spots of blue glaze were dabbed on and the center of each was immediately wiped off lightly.

Terra-cotta over Orange

ABOVE A terra-cotta glaze was brushed over an orange basecoat. This was wiped off by twisting a cloth to create swirls.

Rustic Letter Rack

LEFT This look was created by colorwashing a clear middle-blue glaze over a bright yellow basecoat.

PITFALLS

Colorwashing is usually done by wiping off the glaze in all directions. If you wipe it off in one direction – here, diagonally, (near right) – it looks less even. To achieve depth of color, it is better to apply two thin layers of glaze. If you apply one thick one the effect looks too heavy (far right).

Wiping off in one direction

Glaze too thick

Classical Plaque

RIGHT The plaque was covered with a coat of light gray-brown paint; then a dark glaze made from several shades of brown was painted over it. The surface was wiped over lightly to remove the glaze from the raised areas.

COLOR COMBINATIONS

Dark blue-green on bright green

Brown/mauve on beige

Yellow ocher on warm cream

Middle-blue on pale blue

Colorwashing with a Dado Rail

LEFT The muddy pink basecoat on this wall was colorwashed with dark crimson red glaze above the rail. Below it, the same glaze was used, with a little chocolate brown added.

Colorwashing with a Cornice

LEFT The wall beneath the white cornice has been colorwashed very simply with one layer of raw sienna over an off-white basecoat.

Stippling

THIS CLASSIC TECHNIQUE gives a delicate, sophisticated effect. A thin, almost translucent layer of glaze is applied over the basecoat and hit with a special brush while still wet. The brush breaks up the glaze into small spots – though these can only be seen from close up – allowing the base color to show through. When choosing your colors, make sure that the glaze contains a high concentration of color since it needs to be spread very thinly. Use a white basecoat to show off primary colors, but for more muted shades, off-white may be more suitable. Colored bases will give richer, more complex finishes. Whatever colors you use, stippling works best on very smooth surfaces since it shows up every bump and imperfection.

TOOLS & MATERIALS

Mixed glaze
and brush

*3 x 4in/75 x 100mm
stippling brush for
small areas*

*1 x 4in/25 x 100mm
stippling brush for
corners and details*

*5 x 7in/127 x 178mm
stippling brush for
larger surfaces*

The Basic Technique

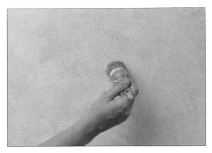

1 Cover the surface with a layer of
glaze, brushing it in all directions
to spread it out very thinly.

2 Go over the surface gently with
the tip of the brush to make it as
smooth and even as possible and to
remove any brushmarks.

3 Using a large stippling
brush, hit the surface with
a steady, strong motion. Move
on to the next area, repeating
the action and overlapping the
previous area each time. The
finished effect should be evenly
and finely speckled.

Dealing with Specks

2 Wipe the stippling brush
regularly with a cloth to
remove the glaze that will
accumulate on the bristles.
Excess glaze on the brush will
spoil the even effect you are
aiming for.

1 Small blobs or specks of glaze
are sometimes left from stippling.
Remove these with your finger and
stipple again immediately.

Stippling a Corner

1 Stipple up to the corner then using a small brush, paint the glaze right into the corner.

2 Stipple one wall as far into the corner as possible without hitting the other wall.

3 Stipple the other wall in the same way. Keep the bristles of the brush parallel to the surface of the wall and wipe off excess glaze from the brush as you work.

4 Using the smallest size stippling brush – 1 x 4in/25 x 100mm – stipple right into the corner, wiping off excess glaze. If you find that too much glaze is being removed, allow the glaze to dry a little before continuing.

Stippling from Light to Dark

1 First apply a band of the lightest colored glaze over the surface, spreading it out thinly and evenly (see The Basic Technique, *p. 39, Steps 1–2).*

2 Leaving a gap below the first band – here 2–3in/ 5–7.5cm – apply another band of the same color in the same way as in Step 1.

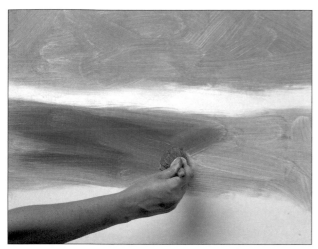

3 While the second (lower) band is still wet, cover it with a second coat of glaze in the darker colored glaze, spreading it out evenly and thinly.

4 Brush the glaze out over the gap to join the darker color to the lighter color above it. Brush well over the edges so that the shades merge. Repeat Steps 2–4 using two layers of the darker colored glaze.

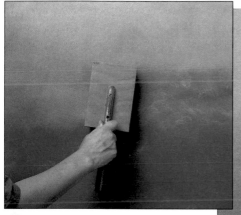

5 Stipple the whole area as directed in The Basic Technique (see p. 39), starting at the top in the lightest area and working downward into the darkest area. Working in this direction ensures that you do not take more glaze back into the paler area. When you have finished (right) the different colored bands should be barely perceptible, with the color just gradually becoming darker towards the bottom.

Stippling a Dado Rail

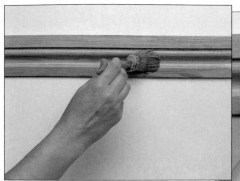

1 Paint the glaze over the rail, taking care to spread it out evenly and not allow too much glaze to accumulate in the crevices.

2 Using a smaller stippling brush – here 3 x 4in/75 x 100mm – stipple evenly along the surface, changing the angle at which you direct the brush to avoid brushmarks. Hold a piece of cardboard against the edge of the rail to protect the wall above and below.

PITFALLS
If you hit the stippling brush too hard on the surface you will create small lines and stripes (near right). Although this is not the classic effect, it could be used as a deliberate technique in itself. If the stippling brush is not hit hard enough against the surface (far right), the brush-marks of the original glaze application will be visible and you will not achieve a satisfactory stippled effect.

Hitting too hard   *Hitting too lightly*

Lamp Base

LEFT This white lamp base was stippled with blue glaze mixed with a little white to lighten it. To get an even finish, you need to stipple the surface delicately and steadily while gradually rotating the lamp base.

COLOR COMBINATIONS

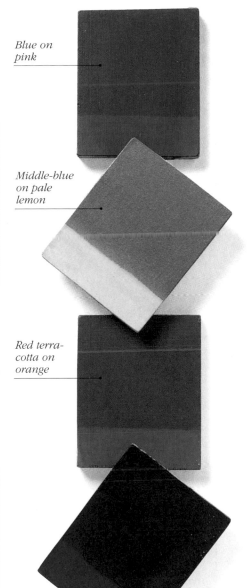

Blue on pink

Middle-blue on pale lemon

Red terra-cotta on orange

Dark green on middle-green

Stippled desk

LEFT AND ABOVE
The dense, velvety texture on this desk was achieved by stippling a cool shade of brown over the warm yellow ocher basecoat. This calm combination suggests natural wood grain.

STIPPLING WITH OTHER BRUSHES

Any brush with short, rigid bristles can be used for stippling with less perfect, but still interesting results. The clusters of bristles in a dustpan brush, for example, leave a noticeable pattern (right).

Clothes brush

Dustpan brush

Stippling with a dustpan brush

Combing

COMBS WERE ORIGINALLY USED for some types of woodgraining, but today are used for many other decorative effects, such as making stripes, checks, and borders. Traditional and contemporary sources can both provide inspiration: tartans, ginghams, madras plaids, and Regency stripes can all suggest stunning color combinations. When combing, the colors you use are more crucial than in other paint effects, which rely on the translucency of the glaze to enhance and deepen the base color. The glaze should be almost completely opaque when combing so that the lines that are created are clear and strong.

Tartan Table

The table was first painted red. When the paint was dry, broad stripes of green glaze were painted across the width of the table and combed with a graduated comb (see Tools and Materials). *When this coat dried, rich blue stripes were painted on in the opposite direction and combed in the same way. Regularly spaced fine lines in pale yellow were painted on to complete the tartan effect.*

TOOLS & MATERIALS

Triangular comb with three different widths of teeth

Graduated comb with two widths of teeth

Glaze

Glazing brush

Rag for wiping glaze off combs

The Basic Technique

1 Paint glaze over the area to be combed, making it as even as possible. If combing a wall, cover an area approximately 3 feet (1 meter) wide, from ceiling to floor.

2 Holding the comb in both hands, with the teeth slanted upward, pull it down carefully from the top. Do it quite quickly to avoid wobbles.

3 If you need to stop halfway, avoid making horizontal lines by lightly relaxing the pressure on the surface before removing the comb.

Double Combing

Homemade (see p. 46) and store bought combs offer teeth with varying widths, both regular and graduated. The possibilities they provide when used in double, triple, or even more layers produce an unlimited variety of combed stripes and checks. Try light, bright colors over dark colors, and vice versa. Below, a graduated comb is used twice to make a checkered pattern.

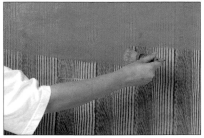

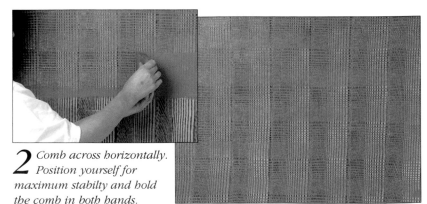

1 Once the previously combed surface has dried completely, cover it with a different colored glaze, spreading it out as evenly as possible.

2 Comb across horizontally. Position yourself for maximum stabilty and hold the comb in both hands.

Making a Comb

While it is possible to buy long-lasting, strong but supple combs, these may not be exactly the right size for your project. You can easily make your own combs using strong cardboard, but they will not last long, since the paper softens and absorbs paint. Soft plastic floor tiles are excellent for homemade combs since they are easy to cut but durable.

1 Cut a rectangular shape in a flexible plastic floor tile. Mark the edge at regular intervals according to the width of tooth and spacing you want.

2 Draw a pencil line parallel to the edge and then draw "V" shapes between every second mark with the base of the "V" facing inward.

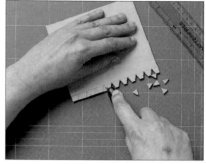

3 Carefully cut out the "V" shapes with a sharp knife, leaving blunted teeth.

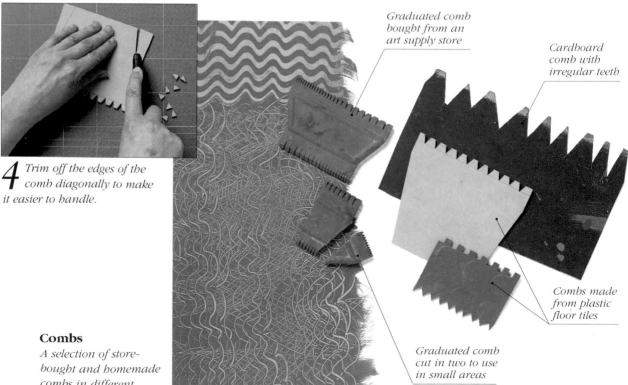

4 Trim off the edges of the comb diagonally to make it easier to handle.

Combs
A selection of store-bought and homemade combs in different materials and sizes.

Graduated comb bought from an art supply store

Cardboard comb with irregular teeth

Combs made from plastic floor tiles

Graduated comb cut in two to use in small areas

Checkerboard Combing

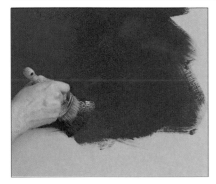

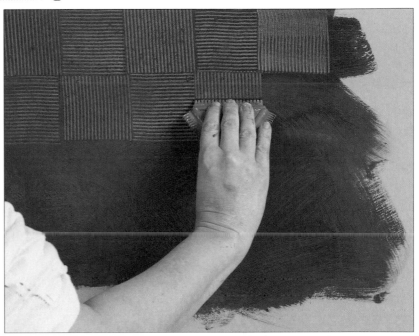

1 Apply the glaze with a brush, spreading it out well. The glaze should contain enough paint to make it opaque.

2 Using a comb with broad, regularly spaced teeth, make alternate vertically and horizontally combed squares (right).

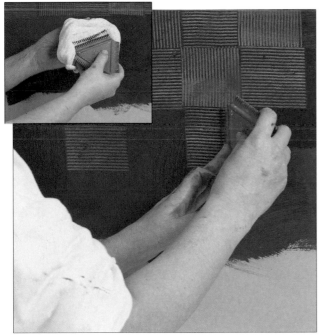

3 Wipe off excess glaze at frequent intervals. After a couple of rows you may find it easier and quicker to comb all the horizontal squares in a row, leaving gaps between them.

4 Complete the pattern by combing vertical squares in the remaining gaps. Instead of squares you could also make diamond shapes by using the comb diagonally.

Alternatives

A vast range of effects can be produced by combing. The size of teeth, direction of the strokes, and color combinations can all be varied with interesting results.

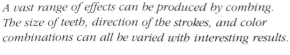

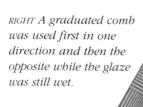

RIGHT A graduated comb was used first in one direction and then the opposite while the glaze was still wet.

ABOVE Different effects were obtained on this blue glaze over a white basecoat, using combs with different size teeth.

ABOVE Green glaze was painted and combed over a red background. When dry, bright blue was combed across in the opposite direction.

LEFT Brown glaze on off-white was combed in a random criss-cross way on the top part of the wall. Underneath, bright blue glaze on terra-cotta was combed leaving regular gaps.

PITFALLS

The right consistency of glaze is critical for achieving the characteristic sharp contrast and smooth lines of combing. If the glaze is too thick (near right), the lines will be blurred, indistinct, and form ridges; if it is too thin (far right), the effect will be thin and watery. To check the consistency of glaze practice on a small area first.

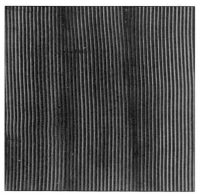

Glaze too thick

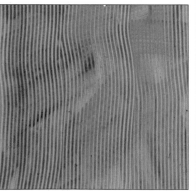

Glaze too thin

COLOR COMBINATIONS

Dark brown on bright green

Bright red on dark blue

White on bright blue

Light gray-green on dark green

Blue and Yellow Table

TOP, ABOVE AND RIGHT This small table was combed with several patterns to give a lively effect. Yellow glaze was applied in selected areas over blue paint and each leg was given a different treatment. A large area on top was left unglazed to heighten the impact of the combed pattern.

Chest of Drawers

LEFT A small drawer unit was painted all over in deep blue-black. White glaze was painted on the drawers and combed with a homemade comb the same width as the drawers. Alternate drawers were combed again to make a strong but irregular vertical stripe. On the remaining drawers the first layer was left to dry, and a second layer of white glaze was combed on horizontally to make a checkered pattern.

Wooden Chest

LEFT A simple wooden chest was painted soft mauve, then combed over with a graduated comb in a darker brown-purple. The subtle effect suggests woodgraining.

Dragging & Flogging

D RAGGING AND FLOGGING ARE two techniques that derive from wood-graining. They replicate this effect when carried out in appropriate wood-toned colors. When used with more varied colors they are decorative techniques in their own right, traditionally used on both plaster walls and woodwork. Historically, dragging was used from the ceiling to the dado rail, with marbled or stippled panels below. There is a subtle difference between the two finishes: dragging produces smooth stripes, while the flogging breaks up the stripes and creates a more uniform overall effect.

Kitchen Cupboard

Contrasting colors and techniques were used to decorate this simple kitchen cupboard. The top drawer front and door panels were painted light blue. Green glaze was dragged over this along the longest dimension. When dry, a second layer of the same green glaze was dragged at right angles to the first stripe. The remaining areas were painted middle-blue and darker blue glaze was dragged over it.

DRAGGING IN CLOSE-UP

Dragging uses a long, coarse-bristled brush and produces a pattern of broken stripes of different lengths. Brush widths range from 2½ to 12 in/62½ to 300 mm. Dragging on plaster walls is done vertically, but on wood it should follow the grain.

TOOLS & MATERIALS

Glaze brush

Dragging brush

Cloth for wiping off glaze

Mixed glaze

The Basic Technique: Dragging

1 Paint on the glaze, spreading it out evenly. Paint vertically in strips to obtain uniform coverage.

2 Brush out the glaze as much as possible to create a thin glaze layer. The surface should not feel sticky.

3 Using the dragging brush, draw the brush up and down, holding it almost parallel to the surface. This will give an even, vertical stripe. The effect should be smooth and without ridges. Leave a wet edge to work into later.

4 To soften the effect hold the brush at almost 90 degrees to the surface and brush up and down at a slight angle to the stripes.

5 Continue on the next strip, working the glaze into the previous wet edge and repeat Steps 3–4 until you have covered the whole surface.

Dragging a Door

Treat the parts of the door in the order they are numbered above. Always drag in the same direction as the grain of the wood.

1 Start applying the glaze in the top center stile (number 1 on the door). Stiles are vertical and rails horizontal.

2 Thoroughly spread out the glaze as evenly as possible, for a smooth and uniform coverage.

3 With a dragging brush, drag the glaze down over the whole top center stile and onto the rail.

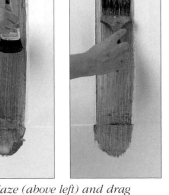

4 Glaze (above left) and drag (above right) the bottom center stile (number 2 on the door).

6 *Finally treat the two outer stiles (numbers 6 and 7), which extend the whole length of the door, making a neat join with the rails.*

5 *Starting at the top of the door, paint the glaze horizontally on the rails (numbers 3, 4, and 5) then drag across. Take care to leave a neat edge against the already dragged stiles.*

Dragging Below a Cornice

1 *When applying the glaze, leave an unglazed gap at the top of the wall near the cornice so the glaze will not be too heavy at this spot. Spread out the glaze vertically with the dragging brush.*

2 *Having wiped excess glaze off the brush on a paper towel (inset), hold the brush against the wall just below the cornice or rail, and apply a little pressure to the tip with the edge of your hand. This will release enough glaze to spread up to the top of the wall.*

Dragging with a Cloth

1 *Paint a contrasting glaze on the surface where a base color has already been applied.*

2 *Pull a bunched-up soft cloth across the surface in a straight line without stopping in the middle.*

Cloth Dragged Table

ABOVE This alternative method of dragging gives a very soft effect. It may be difficult to keep the lines straight, but aligning them visually with an edge and always working in the same direction will help.

Dragging with a Flogging Brush

A flogging brush is used in the same way as the dragging brush but produces a more pronounced striped effect. This can be particularly effective on furniture, and where the colors chosen are close in tone.

PITFALLS

When insufficient pressure is applied to the brush you will not achieve evenly striped dragging and the glaze will be patchy. If you bend your arm as you pull the brush down you will create a curved stroke. To avoid this, make shorter strokes so you can keep your arm straight. Mentally align the brush itself with a straight edge, rather than watching the mark left by it.

Not enough pressure

Curved stripes

COLOR COMBINATIONS

Dark green on bright green

Terra-cotta on bright pink

Off-white on varnished wood

Black on bright red

Chest of Drawers

ABOVE A bright emerald base color had black glaze dragged over it. This toned down the brightness of the green and the contrast between the two colors has given a slightly antiqued look to this chest.

Tartan Effect

ABOVE Terra-cotta and blue stripes were dragged over an egg-yolk yellow basecoat. The stripes are the same width as the brush.

Dragging a Wall

LEFT A red terra-cotta glaze was dragged over a greenish-gray basecoat. Since the colors are close in tone, the result is even and subtle.

The Basic Technique: Flogging

Flogging brushes have much longer bristles than dragging brushes. These produce a light stripe broken up by many small swirls. The final effect is linear, like dragging, but the stripes are broken up and more subtle. As with dragging, flogging on walls is done vertically but on wood it follows the grain.

TOOLS & MATERIALS

Flogging brush

Glaze brush

Mixed glaze

1 Apply the glaze, spreading it out thinly with the brush to form an even layer. As in dragging, paint in vertical strips to obtain uniform coverage.

2 Direct the flogging brush up and down over the glaze to emphasize the striped effect. The surface should be a little wetter than when dragging. Leave an unflogged wet edge to join the next strip.

3 Wipe off excess glaze from the brush. Starting at the bottom and using a sharp action, hit the surface with the top 2–3in/ 50–75mm of the brush, moving up about ¼in/6.25mm each time.

Flogging with Feathers

A blue glaze was thinly painted over a yellow ocher background, and hit with a bunch of feathers, starting at the base and moving upward. This gives a more random result than using a brush. Use any feathers that are long, strong, and fairly flexible – pheasant and peacock feathers for example.

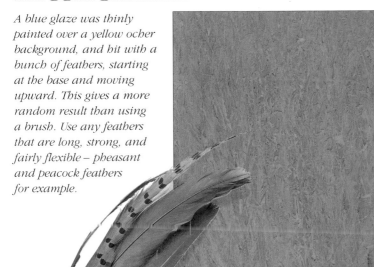

COLOR COMBINATIONS

Black on dark pink

Gray on gray-blue

Pale yellow on blue-green

Terra-cotta on primrose yellow

Flogged Stool

BELOW *An olive green glaze was flogged with a brush over a pale cream basecoat to match the fabric of the seat.*

Decorative Shelf

ABOVE *This gothic-inspired shelf with its integral decorative bracket was flogged, using a brush, in middle-brown over a dark cream basecoat. This gives a subtle suggestion of the grain of wood without trying to imitate wood too accurately.*

Patterning with Cloth

**Cloth Patterned Wall
and Frame**

*The bright yellow wall and
viridian green frame were
covered with orange-terra-
cotta glaze and dark blue-
green glaze respectively,
and then patterned with
cheesecloth/mutton cloth to
give it a lightly mottled look.*

THIS TECHNIQUE GIVES a cloudy, softly mottled finish. The fabric used is
a fine-gauge, slightly elastic cotton knit. It is formed into a rounded
pad by rolling the fabric and then tucking the ends inside the roll.
The pad must be absolutely smooth since any folds in the fabric will make
lines in the glaze. The delicate print of the weave is left on the glazed
surface, creating a deliberately slightly uneven texture. To emphasize this,
the pad can be dabbed more firmly in some areas than others. With careful
application of glaze and even dabbing, the effect can be almost as regular
as that made by stippling.

TOOLS & MATERIALS

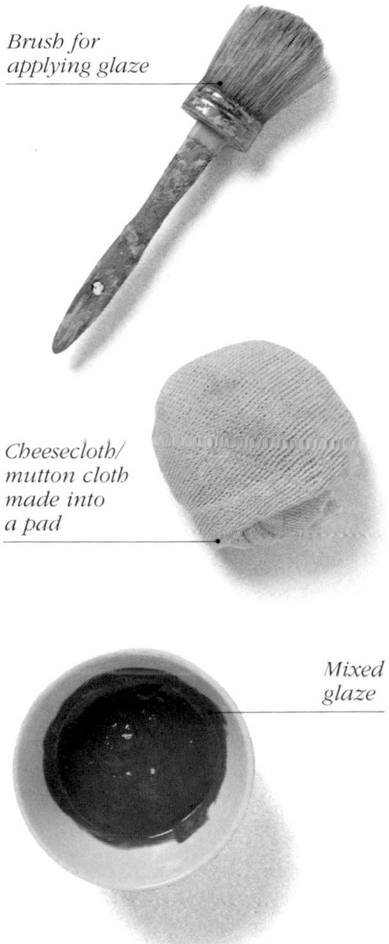

The Basic Technique

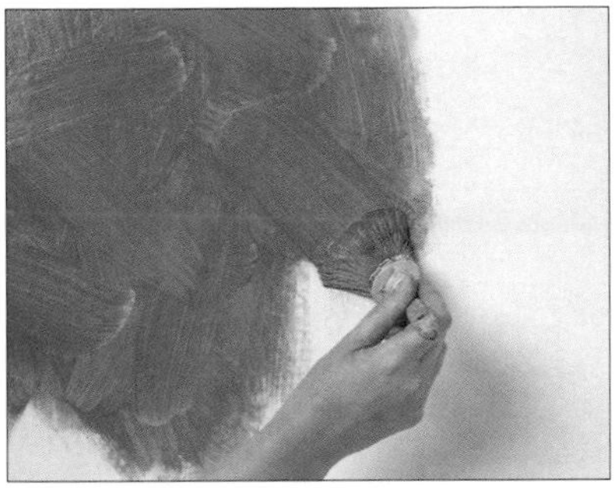

1 Paint the glaze on generously. Use a strongly colored glaze to avoid patchiness, as the cheesecloth/mutton cloth will absorb the paint unevenly.

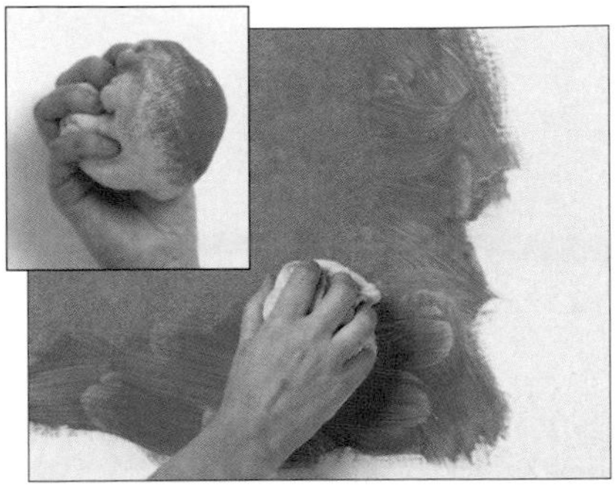

2 Fold the cheesecloth/mutton cloth into a smooth pad. Dab it firmly over a small area. Move quickly on to the next area so the dabs overlap.

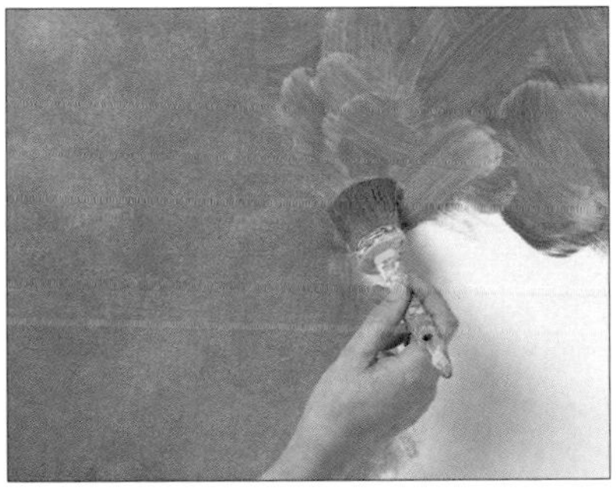

3 Brush more glaze into the wet edge to prepare a new area for patterning. Spread out the paint evenly and brush well into the previous area.

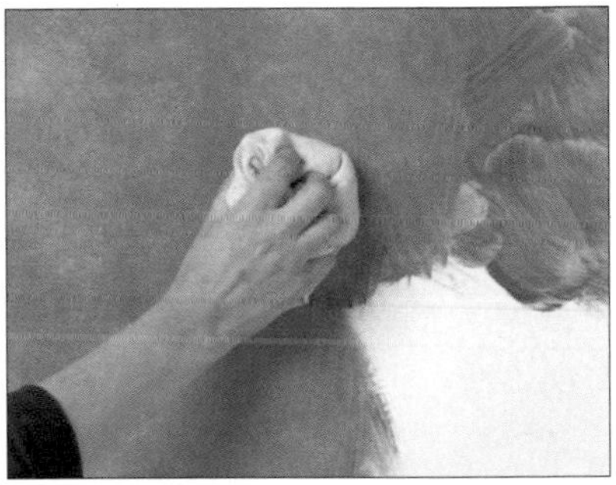

4 Continue dabbing carefully. When the pad is saturated with glaze, turn or refold it to a clean surface to avoid reapplying glaze to the surface.

How to Tear a Cheesecloth/Mutton Cloth

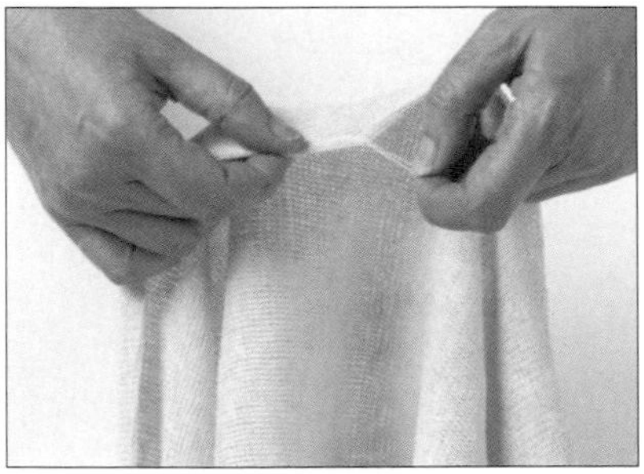

1 To avoid using scissors, which create small threads that stick to the work, pull the end of a thread running the width of the fabric.

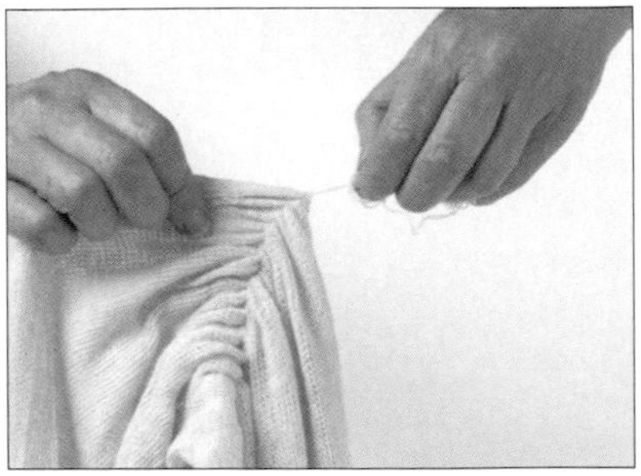

2 While holding the thread, push the gathered fabric along it until the thread either breaks or is pulled out.

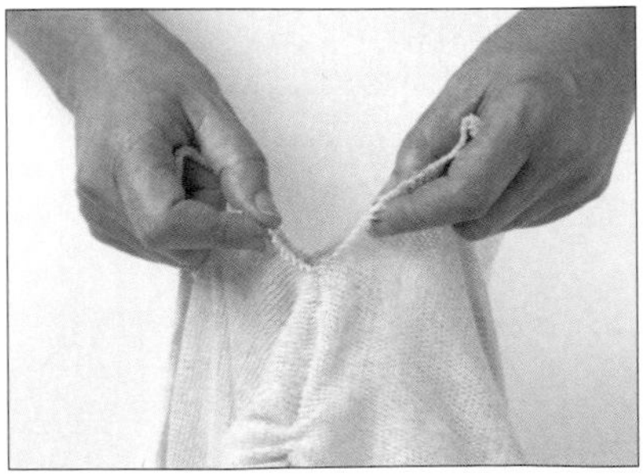

3 The cloth can now be pulled apart and there are no raw ends to ravel.

Patterning a Corner with Cloth

1 Paint the glaze on both walls and into the corner. Avoid letting too much glaze accumulate in the angle.

2 Fold the cloth to make a small edge that fits right into the corner without removing glaze from the other wall.

Creating a Mottled Effect

1 Brush on the glaze, covering the surface well using bold, uneven strokes.

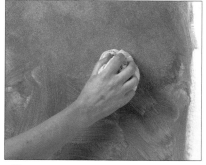

2 Having folded the cheesecloth/ mutton cloth into a smooth pad, dab it all over the surface.

3 Refold the pad to a clean part, then dab patches of the surface again to remove more glaze from some areas than others.

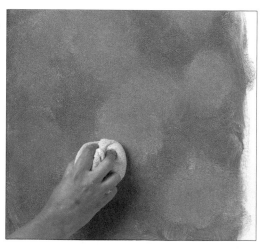

ALTERNATIVES

You can use other types of cloth to create different effects depending on the weave.
A cloth with a coarser weave will produce a more textured look (below).

The sky effect (bottom) was produced by painting blue glaze unevenly over a white basecoat. After cloth patterning all over the surface, use a clean cloth to remove more glaze in patches, suggesting clouds.

Using a coarse-weave cloth

Sky effect

COLOR COMBINATIONS

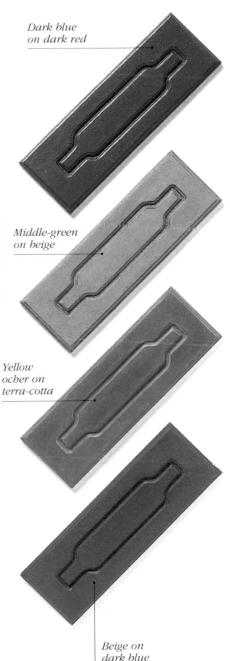

Dark blue on dark red

Middle-green on beige

Yellow ocher on terra-cotta

Beige on dark blue

Cloth Patterned Fireplace

ABOVE AND RIGHT Olive green glaze on a brown-gray basecoat was dabbed off with cheesecloth/ mutton cloth. A smaller piece of cloth was used to clean areas where too much glaze settled.

Cloth Patterned Frame

LEFT The delicate finish on this frame picks up the colors in the picture. A deep mustard ocher glaze was applied over a dark green basecoat and evenly patterned.

PITFALLS

If the glaze is dabbed off unevenly the brushmarks will still show in some areas. Dabbing needs to be done systematically and evenly. If too little pressure is applied the same problem of visible brushstrokes will occur.

Uneven dabbing

Rag Rolling

Rag-Rolled Chest of Drawers

Both stippling and rag rolling were used here. The top, drawers and sides (not visible) were painted pale blue and the rest a darker blue. An even darker blue glaze was then stippled over the whole chest and the drawers and side panels rag rolled to reveal the lighter blue.

AG ROLLING PRODUCES SUBTLE and complex-looking effects because it involves two paint techniques. First the surface is stippled (see pp. 38–43). The layer of glaze is hit firmly with a stippling brush, creating an even effect, then, while the glaze is still wet, a crumpled rag is rolled over it. This removes some of the glaze and reveals the base color. The delicacy of the stippling combined with the light, informal texture of the rag rolling is particularly elegant, especially when two soft, harmonizing colors of similar hue are chosen. More dramatic, contrasting combinations can be effective too. When rag rolling walls, it is quicker and easier for two people to work together. One person can apply and stipple the glaze over a floor to ceiling strip, while the other follows and does the rag rolling.

RAG ROLLING IN CLOSE-UP

This close-up view clearly shows the characteristic texture achieved by rag rolling. The pattern created by rolling off the glaze with the cloth makes the painted surface resemble crumpled fabric.

TOOLS & MATERIALS

Glaze brush

Mixed glaze

Stippling brush

Cotton rag

The Basic Technique

1 First apply the glaze evenly, spreading it out as much as possible. Then hit the surface firmly with the stippling brush (see p. 39), covering a small patch at a time and overlapping as you move on. Leave a wet edge to work into later.

2 Crumple a cotton cloth as for ordinary ragging (see p. 23). Do not form it into a smooth shape.

4 If gaps are left by the rolling process, you can dab over them with the cloth to make the pattern more even.

3 Holding the cloth firmly but not tightly, roll it upward. Leave an area of stippling to join with the next stippling band.

Rag Rolling a Corner

1 Roll the crumpled rag up the wall as near to the corner as possible but without rubbing glaze off the other wall.

2 Using a corner of the rag (or a smaller piece of cloth), dab right into the angle. Press lightly to avoid removing too much glaze.

RAG ROLLING WITH CHAMOIS LEATHER

Chamois leather, a very soft and absorbent material, leaves a strong and distinct pattern. Used wet, it creates a more definite pattern. Used dry, a chamois gives a softer, more muted look. The results of both are shown below – attractively textured surfaces resembling crushed velvet.

Using a dry chamois

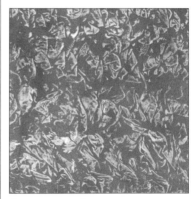

Using a wet chamois

Storage Unit

ABOVE Rag rolling can be used to create a lively, contemporary look. Onto five bright, sharp base colors – orange, red, yellow, green, and blue – a clear blue glaze was stippled then rag rolled. The glaze layer successfully unites the different base colors.

Wastepaper Basket

LEFT The basket was painted a strong, deep red inside and out. Olive green glaze was stippled and rag rolled on the outside. The rich colors are particularly suited to the traditional style of the container.

Rag Rolled Wall

RIGHT The wall was painted dark green, then a pale green glaze was rag rolled in stripes, leaving a narrow strip of dark green visible in between.

Hexagonal Box

BELOW AND BELOW RIGHT The same yellow was used as the base color of both the box and its lid, uniting the two. Bright scarlet was then rag rolled on the lid and warm chocolate glazes on the box.

COLOR COMBINATIONS

Middle-green on yellow ocher

Yellow ocher on dark red

Blue-green on pale green

Terra-cotta red on beige

PITFALLS

As you roll up the walls, the cloth may slip, wiping off a patch of glaze. Avoid this by working over a small area at a time. To correct it, apply a little glaze over the bare patch, stipple it, and dab off with a cloth.

The degree of contrast between glaze color and base color is critical in rag rolling. The dark green stippling (below) is too harsh against the white base; a softer, paler glaze color would have looked better.

Smears

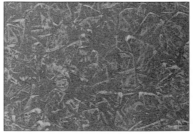

Tonal Contrast

Frottage

THIS PAINT EFFECT IS achieved without glaze. Instead you apply watered-down paint over a dry painted surface and lay paper or a similar absorbent material over the wet paint, flattening it out with your hands. Some of the paint is absorbed by the paper. When the paper is removed, a random pattern of paint is left. Each new sheet of paper and fresh layer of paint produces a different effect. Although the characteristic look of frottage is achieved primarily by chance, there are ways in which it can be controlled. The absorbency of the base paint, the choice of colors and the length of time the paper is left on are all factors influencing the end result.

Frottaged Wall

Slate blue was frottaged over an olive brown basecoat. Frottage tends to produce an irregular effect, as here, with the base color showing through more clearly in some places than others.

FROTTAGE IN CLOSE-UP

Part of the unique texture produced by frottage is the small lines that are created by the "grain" of the newspaper.

TOOLS & MATERIALS

Brush for applying paint

Mixed paint

Newspaper

The Basic Technique

1 Mix the paint to the required consistency: it should be approximately two-thirds paint to one-third water. The mix may have to be adjusted according to the type of paint and the surface. Hold the newspaper up to the wall and mark the area it covers.

2 Cover the marked out area with a fairly generous amount of paint. Work quickly before it dries out.

3 Lay a sheet of newspaper over the wet painted surface. Smooth all over with the palm of your hands, taking care to apply even pressure so you will not leave hand prints.

4 Peel off the paper carefully with one hand while still holding it in place with the other.

Joining Frottage Areas

1 Move on to the next area, applying the paint up to the edge of the finished area.

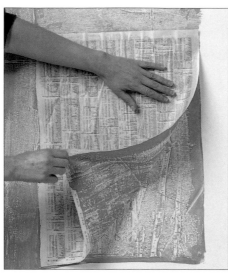

2 Place the paper down on the newly painted surface and then remove it as in steps 3 and 4 of the Basic Technique.

3 There are dark lines where each new frottaged area begins. To hide these, use double frottage (see opposite).

PITFALLS

When there is a too strong a color contrast between the basecoat and the topcoat, the effect is somewhat coarse (below left): for a more subtle effect choose two colors closer in tone. It is also very important that the topcoat is of the right consistency. If you dilute it with too much water the paint will become very runny, resulting in visible drips in some areas (below center). If very little water is added the effect is very dense and heavy, losing the typical texture of frottage (below right).

Colors too strong

Too much water added

Too little water added

Double Frottage

The reason why you might choose double frottage is to change the color effect and also either to emphasize or camouflage the shapes left by the paper. As you can see, this technique builds up a richly textured surface and offers endless opportunities for variations.

1 Coat a small part of your frottaged surface with diluted paint in a contrasting color. You can cover a larger area once you learn how quickly the paint dries.

2 Tear off irregularly shaped and sized pieces of newspaper and lay them over the whole of the painted area while it is still wet.

3 Smooth your hands all over the paper to ensure even contact with the paint.

4 Peel off the paper. The finished effect shows how the regular rectangles and straight lines of the first paint layer have been hidden. Lines where one patch ends are inevitable to some extent, but can be minimized by using, as here, regularly shaped pieces of paper for the first layer and irregularly shaped pieces for the second layer only.

FROTTAGE WITH OTHER MATERIALS

Crumpled tissue paper gives a smaller, more even pattern than newspaper. Here (below), blue was frottaged over a red basecoat. Finely woven cotton was used to frottage the warm orange-brown and green, and blue stripes over the pale orange basecoat (right).

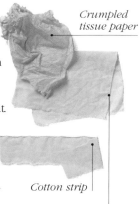

Crumpled tissue paper

Cotton strip

Piece of cotton

Frottage with tissue paper

Frottage with fabric and three colors

Double Frottage

ABOVE *Reddish brown paint was frottaged over a grayish brown basecoat. To soften the effect yellow ocher was frottaged over this.*

Hanging Box

ABOVE *The warm yellow ocher basecoat and rich terracotta topcoat complement each other well on this box. Pieces of paper were torn to the correct width in order to frottage inside the compartments.*

COLOR COMBINATIONS

Dark blue on bright red

Frottaged Desk

LEFT AND BELOW Rich dark green was painted and then frottaged over a deep red basecoat. The dark colors suit the classic shape of the desk and give a convincingly antique effect, as shown in the close-up.

Off-white on light blue

Dark green on turquoise blue

Frottaging a Chair

LEFT AND ABOVE The chair was painted a strong, bright orange and then frottaged over with a cooler blue paint. The bold, strongly contrasting colors give the chair a lively modern look, showing how versatile this technique can be.

Dark red on blue-green

Woodgraining

Woodgrained Chair

A simple, 1930s-style chair was given a maple-effect grain by using a warm, ginger-colored glaze over a yellow ocher basecoat. The baseboard was grained to match. The close-up detail shows how a darker glaze on the center panel gives a more pronounced grain.

USING PAINT TO IMITATE wood is a very old craft. It has probably been practiced for 200 years using the same techniques as today. Although wood can seem intimidating, it is not really a difficult technique. The wood effects shown here, mahogany, oak, and maple, exemplify a range of basic techniques and illustrate the use of essential tools. Once the basics are mastered, these skills can be adapted to reproduce numerous other woods. Achieving a convincing finish can seem quite daunting, but accurate color makes an enormous difference to the result and so careful study of real wood will pay off. Using the correct tools will also help, but you may prefer to try out some of the techniques with adapted tools and brushes before investing.

TOOLS & MATERIALS

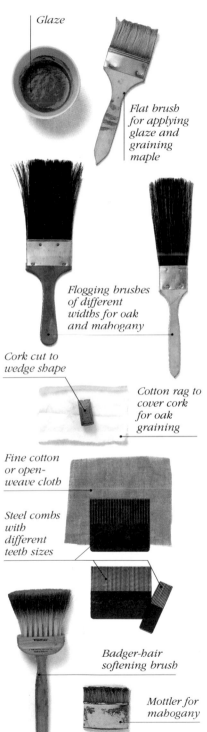

Glaze

Flat brush
for applying
glaze and
graining
maple

Flogging brushes
of different
widths for oak
and mahogany

Cork cut to
wedge shape

Cotton rag to
cover cork
for oak
graining

Fine cotton
or open-
weave cloth

Steel combs
with
different
teeth sizes

Badger-hair
softening brush

Mottler for
mahogany

Mahogany Graining

Mahogany graining is best used on surfaces that are large enough to show the characteristic arch-shaped heart or "flame" to its best advantage. The sample below shows a warm, deep red mahogany, an effect which is recreated by painting dark chocolate brown glaze over a dark reddish-pink basecoat.

1 Paint on the glaze vertically with a flat brush. Spread it out so the basecoat is visible (inset). Using a dry flogging brush, tap the bristles at 1 in/25 mm intervals, working up from the bottom.

2 Dry off the flat brush. Create a half arch shape by moving the sides of the bristles in a wavy diagonal. Move up in successive arches, varying the pressure (but not too regularly) to resemble light and dark grain.

3 To vary the shapes you make, twist the brush so that the bristles are at right-angles to the surface.

4 Pull the mottler down in some areas, following the arch shape. Vary pressure to make darker and lighter marks, imitating mahogany's undulating grain.

Oak Graining

To show off the beauty of oak graining you need a fairly large area, such as a door. The finish is easier to achieve on a flat or only slightly curved surface. Oak graining can look cool and delicate when you use creams and grays, or warm when rich or dark brown glazes are chosen. For the middle-brown color shown below, use burnt umber glaze over a cream basecoat.

1 *Work in panels about 18in/45cm wide and 1 or 2 yards/1–2 meters high – like planks of real wood – according to the area being covered. Apply the glaze vertically with a flat brush.*

2 *Fold a piece of fine cotton or open-weave cloth around a wide-toothed metal comb, tucking the edges in so that it is easy to handle.*

3 *Pull the covered comb downward in a vertical line, twisting it very slightly to left and right to achieve the wavy look of real wood.*

4 *While the glaze is still wet, go over the surface with a finer-toothed comb. Work at a slight diagonal to break up the vertical lines and make the light "dashes" typical of oak grain.*

Graining with a Cork

1 You can imitate the small half-arch shapes that appear on oak by using a cork. Sharpen a cork to a wedge shape and wrap it in a cloth.

2 Draw small half-arch shapes, making them look random by pressing harder at first, then relaxing the pressure. Group them together in areas and leave other patches free. Study real oak to see where these marks occur so you can reproduce them convincingly.

Maple Graining

This is a soft, delicate effect, particularly good on small items such as frames, boxes, and lamp bases. Below, a light, warm brown glaze is used over a honey-colored basecoat. For a richer look, a yellow ocher basecoat could be used, or a pink-toned basecoat with a chocolate brown glaze. This technique can be adapted to achieve a satinwood or rosewood effect.

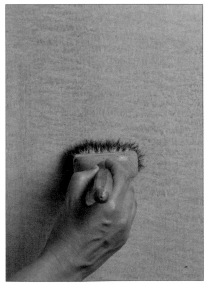

1 Apply the glaze in one direction with a flat brush, spreading it out so the basecoat shows through.

2 While the glaze is still wet, gently twist a mottler from side to side while moving it over the surface. Press on the bristles when changing direction to release more glaze, giving spots of color typical of maple.

3 Before the glaze is dry brush over the surface with a softening brush to blend in the darker areas. Do not make the color too uniform. You can omit this stage if you like the effect already achieved.

Woodgraining Alternatives

The details show oak graining (right) on pale gray, with darker gray glaze; bird's-eye maple (below) in rich, warm colors with minimum contrast between tones; and walnut graining (below right) in paler, colder colors, here, cool brown on greenish-yellow ocher.

Oak graining (above)

Maple graining (above)

Walnut graining (right)

Grained Tabletop

RIGHT This elegant tabletop shows maple graining used to simulate different wood veneers. Different shades of brown glaze were used and it was softened on the paler areas to recreate the look of satinwood. The black banding and stenciled motif imitate ebony effectively.

Tall Shelf Unit

ABOVE This unit is made from old, rough wood. Its rustic look was emphasized by the deliberately strong contrast between the reddish-pink basecoat and the brown glaze, which was deepened with a little dark blue.

Decorative Wooden Case

BELOW The main panel was grained to imitate burr walnut with dark brown glaze over an orange basecoat. The central motif was stenciled on and glaze was dabbed on and blended, using a softening brush, to resemble satinwood. The outer band was initially treated using the mahogany technique and adapted to imitate rosewood.

Coal Bucket

ABOVE This old metal coal bucket has a new lease of life as a decorative object with an oak grain treatment, a typical Victorian effect. At that time metal was beginning to replace wood for many domestic items, but since it was an unfamiliar material it was often disguised to look like wood.

PITFALLS

Important tips for achieving convincing wood finishes are to judge the colors carefully and to mix a translucent glaze that will not mask the base color. In the example (below left) too little glaze has been used over the basecoat, so the effect is dull and opaque. The detail (below center) shows the crude result when the glaze color and basecoat contrast too sharply. The example (below right) shows how unrealistic graining looks when the brushmarks are painted too evenly.

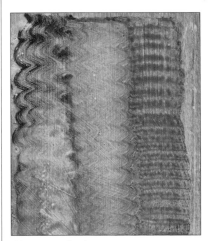

Not enough glaze

Wrong colored basecoat

Brush marks too regular

Decorative Graining

Decoratively Grained Wall

This boldly colored modern room uses almost complementary shades of scarlet and blue to dramatic effect. Gray-blue glaze was grained with the "oak" edge of the roller (see p. 80).

WITH WOODGRAINING the intention is to imitate natural wood as closely as possible. However, you can also achieve a colorful and decorative effect with different types of flexible combs and rollers. The purpose is not to create a totally convincing replica, but to produce the look of painted oak and pine quickly and easily. The same method can be used to simulate moiré silk or other fabrics. You can experiment with overlaying patterns and colors, remembering that this technique is more suited to bold than subtle effects.

TOOLS & MATERIALS

Plastic graining roller with removable head for wide or thin grains

Soft plastic graining comb with two different widths

Glaze

Cloth to wipe off excess glaze from comb and surface

Flogging brush for softening

Brush for applying glaze

The Basic Technique

1 Apply the glaze vertically, brush it out to give a thin translucent covering. Wipe over with a soft cloth so that only a very thin layer of glaze is left.

2 Apply the top of the roller to the glazed surface. Rock the roller halfway down its length to achieve the grained effect, the top of the head gives the broad effect of oak grain.

3 Work down the wall from the top, rocking the roller very slightly at intervals. You may want to use both hands to ensure firm contact with the surface.

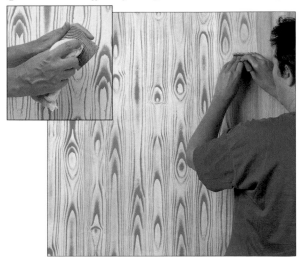

4 Remove excess glaze built up at the top of the head with a soft cloth (inset). You can achieve the narrower effect of pine grain by rocking the roller all the way down and then up again. This produces characteristic circular knot shapes. Space these irregularly.

Softening the Pattern

The grained effect can be left as previously shown, but if you want to heighten the look of moiré silk rather than wood, or simply to make the effect less strong, the finish can be softened with a flogging, dragging, or softening brush. A flogging brush, as used below, emphasizes the fabric effect. This is enhanced even more if a soft color similar to the glaze is used for the base.

Using the flogging brush, lightly pull down the bristles over the thin and still slightly wet glaze. This will blur the edges of the "knots".

To accentuate the look of fabric and soften the effect even more, the flogging brush can be brushed across horizontally as well as vertically.

Different Types of Grain

These pictures (right) show the different surfaces of the graining roller heads and the oak and pine effects they can create.

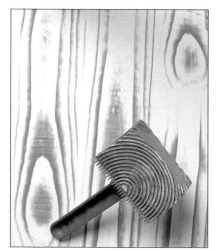

Oak effect

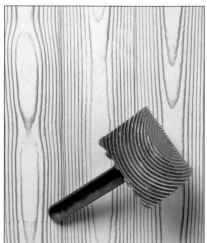

Pine effect

COLOR COMBINATIONS

Brown on beige

Light blue on dark blue

Strong green on clear yellow

Strong pink on bright pink

Bedside Cabinet

LEFT *This small cabinet was painted dark blue and a grayish white glaze was applied over it. The graining comb was used just to make a swirling pattern rather than to imitate wood.*

Picture Frame

ABOVE *Green glaze was painted over a reddish-brown basecoat. Since the comb was wider than the frame, only the middle section of the roller was used. The result is a woodgrained look, but in deliberately unnatural colors.*

PITFALLS

If the glaze is too thick and wet, the graining looks heavy. Here, the color also contrasts too strongly with the white background and the graining is too regular for it to have a natural look. Avoid repeating the rocking motion too often, since it creates unattractive breaks and lines across the grain.

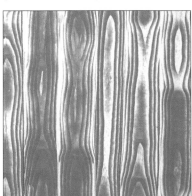

Too heavily lined

Broken grain

Marbling

Marbled Chest

The panels of this chest were marbled using a soft, warm raw sienna deepened with a little raw umber. After the initial layer of glaze was applied, the panels were sponged, ragged, and veined. The surrounds were painted a deep green-blue.

MARBLING, LIKE WOODGRAINING, is a technique in which one material is painted to imitate another. To achieve a convincing result it is important to study examples of real marble. But because real marble comes in so many different colors and patterns, you can work more freely than when woodgraining. Marbling techniques are very flexible. The first step is the subtle blending of softened tones but then other methods, such as sponging, splattering, or veining with artist's brushes or a feather, can be used separately or together. Marbling is traditionally done on structural surfaces, such as walls, floors, and pillars but it can be just as effective on small items, such as lamp bases, boxes, and frames. The finished work should be sealed with gloss or semigloss varnish (see pp. 18–19) both to protect the surface and give it the shiny look of real marble.

TOOLS & MATERIALS

Brush for
applying
glaze

Colored
glaze

Softening
brush

Cheesecloth/
mutton cloth

Water

Denatured alcohol/
methylated spirits

Cotton rag

Swordliner

Rigger

Brush for
splattering

Sponge

Tray for mix-
ing paint
and glaze

Small stippling
brush for use on
moldings

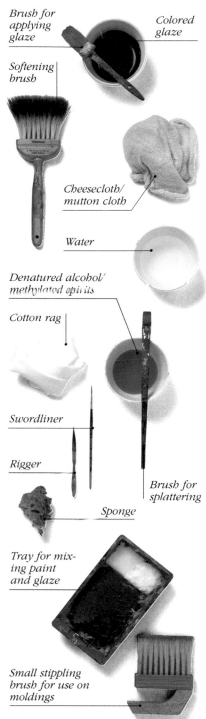

The Basic Technique

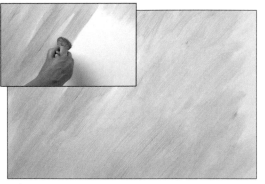

1 Color the glaze, ensuring that it remains
transparent. Mix only a little at a time, this
way the shade of each batch will vary. Apply
the glaze diagonally, varying the angle and
thickness of the brushstrokes.

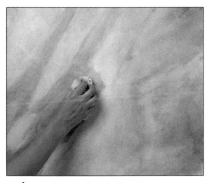

2 Add darker paint to
the glaze and apply it
in patches, strengthening
some of the existing darker
areas. Aim to establish
three tones: light, medium
and dark.

3 Fold cheesecloth/mutton cloth
into a smooth pad and dab the
glaze in the lighter areas to remove
brushstrokes and even out the colors.

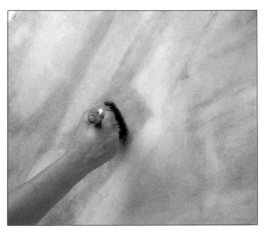

4 Now dab the darker areas.
Treating dark and light areas
separately keeps them well defined
and contrasting.

5 While the glaze is still wet,
use the softening brush to
remove the cheesecloth/
mutton cloth marks. If you let
the glaze dry out you will be
unable to remove them. Hold
the brush at right angles to
the surface and move it from
side to side, using your arm,
not your wrist, to achieve a
smooth effect without creating
visible brushstrokes. You can
then add veins, if desired
(see pp. 84–85).

Veining

It is not essential to add veins to make marbling look realistic, but although tricky to do well, veining can look very effective. Always work around the shapes and colors of the basic marbling, emphasizing and outlining the darker shapes. Veining is done with slightly thinned paint, not glaze, and in a color just a little darker than the base shade. Various tools can be used for veining, including artist's brushes, feathers, and a special brush used just for painting lines called a swordliner. You can use a rigger, a short smaller brush that makes thinner lines, to reduce veins that are too thick.

Using Artist's Brushes

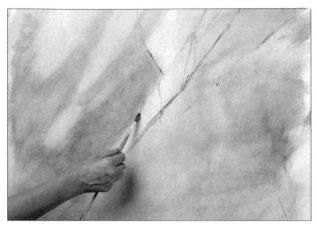

1 Use a small artist's fitch, made of soft bristle, to outline darker areas or create veins of varying thickness. Do not hold the brush like a pencil, but allow it to move loosely so that the veins do not look too tightly drawn.

2 Go over the veins with a softening brush so that they gently blend into the background. Use the brush as in step 5 of The Basic Technique *(see p. 83)*

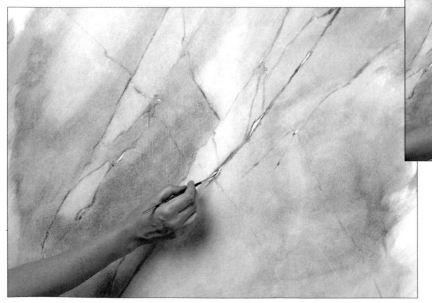

3 Lighten thick areas by dipping a rigger in water and removing a little paint to reveal the white base and form a lighter "island" within a vein (left). This can only be done while the paint is still wet. To soften the effect further, rag the veins gently with a cotton cloth to break up the veining slightly (above).

Using a Swordliner

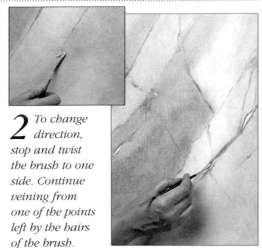

1 Use the tip of the brush to start the vein, then increase the pressure to broaden the line.

2 To change direction, stop and twist the brush to one side. Continue veining from one of the points left by the hairs of the brush.

3 You can add to the veining with a rigger, complementing the shapes made by the swordliner. It is used in the same way – by stopping the line and twisting the brush.

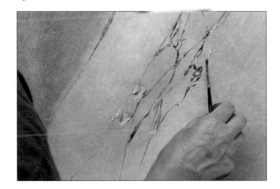

Using a Feather

Any long, strong feathers – such as goose, duck, or peacock – are suitable for veining. Use a feather with the longer barbs on the right for veins starting at the top left, and vice versa. Dip the feather in the paint, dab it on to the surface, then drag across it. Since the feather is curved, this may feel awkward at first, but this method produces authentically irregular veins.

PITFALLS

If you drag the side rather than the tip of the softening brush along the surface you will get scratches (below).

Veining can look crude and artificial for several reasons. Here (bottom), the lines are too dark and positioned arbitrarily, without relating to the dark and light areas in the basecoat. The three lines at the top right are too evenly spaced and the wiggly line looks unnatural. The thickness of the lines is too regular. Veins should start at the side of the work and vary from thick to thin, eventually petering out altogether. Take care not to cross lines, as shown. The meeting point of veins should either form a little "island" or the line should continue on the other side a small distance away from the meeting point.

Scratches

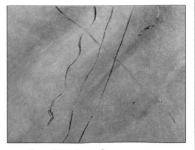

Artificial looking lines

Splatter Marbling

Some natural marbles have a pattern of small spots and few or no veins. Marbling to achieve this kind of effect is useful for small objects where an intense overall look is required. Splatter marbling is a technique that can be used on both horizontal and vertical surfaces and it can be used to cover a whole area or just part of a larger marbled surface to give a bit of variety.

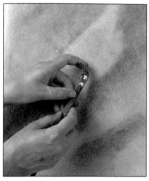

1 While the basecoat is still wet, take a small stiff brush, dip it in water, and using your finger, splatter the water over the surface.

2 Go over the area immediately with a softening brush to reveal the spots made by the water. Do this lightly or the spots will be smoothed out.

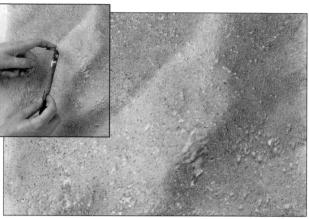

3 For greater depth and variety mix a little darker paint with the water and splatter small areas. Soften gently. The final result is a mixture of light and dark spots of varying sizes.

Marbling a Cornice

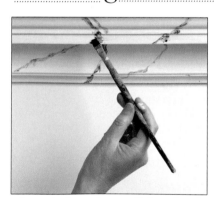

1 Apply thin, clear, or light-colored glaze to the surface, taking care not to let glaze build up in the crevices. Paint on veins in a diagonal direction, varying the thickness of the lines. Apply the paint quite thinly so that the veins do not look heavy.

2 Dab over the veins with a stippling brush along the direction of the line. Wipe the bristles on a cloth from time to time to remove excess paint and glaze. Repeat as necessary until the vein looks soft.

Marbling Panels

1 Real marble comes in slabs. For an authentic look on a wall divide it into suitably sized panels, marking the edges with a soft pencil.

2 Marble a panel, then wipe off any glaze that has spread over the pencil line into the next panel.

3 Marble every other panel and allow it to dry completely, preferably overnight. Then marble the unpainted panels in the same way.

4 Wipe off any glaze that has gone onto the adjacent panel. The pencil line should show through and resemble the gap between slabs. It can be deepened with a darker pencil if desired.

5 To harmonize the panels, you can add in some more veins at this stage, or veins can be darkened, as shown here, to match veining elsewhere.

Floating Marble

Floating marble is a quick and effective technique that you can use on horizontal surfaces, such as tabletops and floors. Here, strong, bright colors are used, but the technique also works particularly well with very dark, more subtle shades such as the greens used on the plaque opposite. You can also do this technique using one color only to give an overall textured effect.

1 Apply one colored glaze in patches, spreading it out well over the surface.

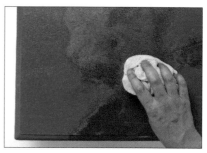

2 Paint the second color on the bare areas. With a smooth pad of folded cheesecloth/mutton cloth dab over first one color, then the other, using a clean part of the pad to avoid mixing and muddying the colors.

3 Go over the whole surface gently with a softening brush to even out the glaze.

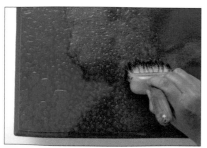

4 Dip the softening brush in water and dab it all over the surface, forming small spots.

5 Next dip the softening brush in denatured alcohol/methylated spirits and dab it over the surface. The combination of glaze, water, and denatured alcohol/methylated spirits will produce spots and blotches of different sizes. Allow the surface to dry without softening it.

Picture Frame

LEFT The floating technique was used here, with water, denatured alcohol/methylated spirits, and paint used alternately to build up layers of spots and patches. The off-white veins were painted on diagonally as if the whole frame were one piece of marble.

Floating Marbling on a Panel

RIGHT Over a white basecoat, blue and terra-cotta glazes created this floating marble surface. This can be used on floors or any other flat surface.

Marbled Plaque

RIGHT AND BELOW This plaster plaque was painted black and then glazed with several shades of dark green, using the floating method to reveal the layers and create spots of different colors.

Sponge Marbling

This technique is particularly suitable for small areas and objects. A sponge is dipped in water and then dabbed over the surface to lift off glaze, leaving lighter spots and blobs. Then darker paint is dabbed on for contrast. Experiment with doing more or less of the two stages to achieve a result you like.

Choose a sponge with large holes so the paint leaves a more positive mark.

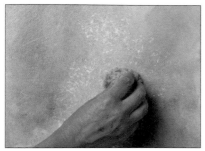

1 Apply the glaze so that there are dark and light areas. While the surface is still wet, dab over the lighter areas with a damp sponge.

2 Thin paint in a slightly darker shade than the glaze color so that it flows freely. Dip a clean sponge in the paint, using a tray so that the sponge can be squeezed out slightly so it is not too saturated. Dab the sponge on the darker areas, lightly at first to judge the effect. More layers can be built up for a more strongly contrasting look.

Candlestick

RIGHT The effect here is of granite, achieved by the sponge method with first gray, then black glaze applied over an off-white basecoat.

Marbled Case

ABOVE AND RIGHT The border was painted to imitate dramatic black and sienna Porto d'Oro marble. The inner panel has a white basecoat painted over with very faint black veins to resemble Carrara marble, then stippled over slightly for a trompe-l'œil look.

Marbled Door

LEFT Over a white basecoat, raw sienna, raw umber, and white were sponge marbled around the edge of this door, and splatter marbled on the inside panel. The effect is light and warm.

COLOR COMBINATIONS

Deep blue-green with white veins on gray

Beige with dark cool brown veins on white

Black veins on trans-parent glaze

White and terra-cotta on black

Cool Gray Mirror

ABOVE This mirror was painted white and splatter marbled with different proportions of ultra-marine blue, raw umber and white, giving a gray-blue looking, cold marble effect.

Splatter Marbled Candlestick

LEFT A wooden candlestick was painted light, cool brown. The splatter technique was then applied using various proportions of raw umber and white. When this coat was dry a second layer using burnt sienna was randomly applied in the same way. The two layers of dark colors give the candlestick a solid, heavy look.

Combining Techniques

U SING DIFFERENT PAINT EFFECTS in combination with one another gives greater emphasis to the different part of the surface. You could marble, stipple, or comb a chair rail or dado rail, and then use a different technique, such as ragging, colorwashing, or patterning with cloth, on the wall above it. In the same way, you can highlight the different parts of a piece of furniture, with one effect on panels or tabletops and another for the panel surrounds or table legs.

Don't combine too many different techniques or they will detract from one another. Two techniques is normal, but on walls and larger furniture, three techniques can be used.

Wall and Dado-rail
Off-white was covered with blue-gray for the colorwashed top and dragged dado, and terra-cotta for the combed area.

*Colorwashing
(pp. 30–37)*

*Dragging
(pp. 50–55)*

*Combing
(pp. 44–49)*

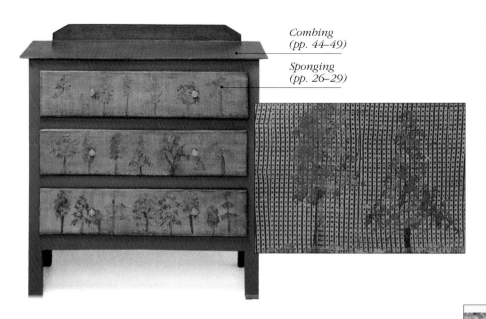

Combing
(pp. 44–49)

Sponging
(pp. 26–29)

Combed and Sponged Chest of Drawers

Olive-green was combed over a red basecoat on the top and drawer fronts of this chest of drawers. The tree shapes were made by sponging on dark green, middle-green, and a little yellow-ocher.

Marbled and Dragged Candlestick

The off-white basecoat was covered with white glaze and then marbled using a variety of blacks and ochers. A charcoal gray was dragged around the base.

Marbling
(pp. 82–91)

Dragging
(pp. 50–55)

Frottaged and Sponged Cupboard

On the center panels, deep cherry pink was frottaged over the pale gray basecoat, while on the surrounds three colors – dark red, dark blue, and dark green were sponged on.

Frottage
(pp. 66–71)

Sponging
(pp. 26–29)

Index

Suppliers

The following suppliers are listed in alphabetical order by county. For more information on Annie Sloan and Annie Sloan's Traditional Paints you can visit her Internet site on www.anniesloan.co.uk

Focus on the Past
Waterloo Street, Clifton, Bristol, Avon, BS8 4BT

Henry Morse
70 Alma Road, Clifton, Bristol, Avon, BS8 2DJ

The Shop Inside Out
High Street, Winford
Bristol, Avon, BS18 7JH

Crafty Ideas
13 High Street, Bedford
Beds, MK40 1RN

Home Makers
Bishop Centre Shopping Village, Bath Road, Taplow, Berks, SL6 0NX

Jeremy Hancock
Fanny's
1 Lynmouth Road, Reading, Berks, RG1 8DD

Paint Effects at Windsor Fireplaces
339 St. Leonards Road, Windsor, Berks, SL4 3DS

The Natural Fabric Co.
Wessex Place
127 High Street, Hungerford
Berks, RG17 0DL

Painted Furniture
Unit 6 Clarence Mill
Bollington, Macclesfield
Cheshire, SK10 5JT

Wrights of Lymm Ltd
Millers Lane, Lymm
Cheshire, WA13 9RG

Cynthia Greenslade
The Granary, Treviskey
Portloe, Truro
Cornwall, TR2 5PN

Rooks Wood Workshop
The Old Vicarage
St. Clether, Nr. Launceston
Cornwall, PL15 8UQ

Decorative Arts
4 Market Place, Melbourne
Derbys, DE73 1DS

The Stencil Shop
Eyam Hall Craft Centre
Eyam, Derbys, SS30 1QW

In-Perspective
46A Meads Street, Eastbourne
East Sussex, BN20 7RG

Woodcare
The Old Granary, Battlesbridge, Essex, SS11 7RF

Bailey Paints
Griffin Mill Estate, London Road, Thrupp, Nr. Stroud
Glos, GL5 7AZ

Country Colours
20 West Way, Cirencester
Glos, GL7 1PY

Jaspers
The Market Place, Northleach, Glos, GL54 3EG

Burwoods
60 The High Street
Lymington, Hants, SO41 9AH

Burwoods
14 The Square, Winchester
Hants, SO23 9ES

Crafty Ideas
6 The Arcade, Hitchin
Herts, SG5 1ED

Dacorum Colour Supplies
2–3 Mark Road, Hemel Hempstead
Herts, HP2 7BN

District Modern Stores
2 Vaughan Road, Harpenden
Herts, AL5 4ED

The Little Country Store
9 High Street, London Colney, St. Albans
Herts, AL2 1RE

Artlines and Outlines
58 Glebe Way, West Wickham, Kent
BR4 0RL

Chromos
59 High Street, Tunbridge Wells, Kent
TN1 1XF

Half a Sixpence
Evegate Craft Centre
Station Road, Evegate
Smeeth, Ashford, Kent, TN25 6SX

Stencil Essentials at The Mad Hatters
26 High Street, Otford
Kent, TN14 5PQ

Pam Zahler
Lane House, Fowgill
Bentham, Lancs, LA2 7AH

Foxwell & James
57 Farringdon Road
London, EC1M 3JH

Anne le Painter at Jeanne Forbes
4 Shillingford Street
London, N1 2DP

A S Handover Ltd.
37H Mildmay Grove
London, N1 4RH

Harris Fine Art
712 High Road
North Finchley
London, N12 9QD

Crisp and Hodgson
165 Cricklewood Broadway
London, NW2 3HT

Vargail DIY and Paints
303–305 Cricklewood Lane
London, NW2 2JL

M P Moran & Son
299–301 Kilburn High Road, London, NW6 7JS

S & S Home Supplies Ltd
16–18 Hale Lane, Mill Hill
London, NW7 3NX

Morse
264 Lee High Road
London, SE13 5PL

Mylands
80 Norwood High Street
London, SE27 9NW

Paint Service Co. Ltd.
19 Eccleston Street
London, SW1W 9LX

Green and Stone
259 Kings Road
London, SW3 5EL

The Decorating Centre Ltd.
2 Filmer Road
London, SW6 7BT

Colour Sensation
52 Gloucester Road
London, SW7 4QB

Michael Putman
151 Lavender Hill
London, SW11 5QJ

Conkers Arts and Crafts
26 Tooting Bec Road
London, SW17 8BD

Wheatsheaf Graphics
54 Baker Street
London, W1M 1DJ

Lords Trade and DIY
119–121 Westbourne Grove
London, W2 4UP

Interiors of Chiswick
454–458 Chiswick High
Road, London
W4 5TT

Omni Home Ltd.
77 Golborne Road
London, W10 5NP

Askew Paint Centre
103 Askew Road
London, W12 9AS

**Neale Robinson Trade
Supplies**
191A Uxbridge Road
London, W12 9RA

London Graphic Centre
16–18 Shelton Street
London, WC2H 9JJ

Allpro Services
14–15 Station Parade
Northolt Road, South
Harrow, Middx, HA2 8HB

Paints 'n' Papers
394 Long Lane, Hillingdon
Middlesex, UB10 9PG

S & S Home Supplies Ltd.
389–391 Honeypot Lane
Stanmore, Middx, HA7 1JJ

The Triumph Press
91 High Street, Edgware
Middx, HA8 7OB

Sloane's Emporium
8-10 Shore Street
Killyleagh, Co. Down
N Ireland, BT30 9QJ

Paint & Paper Ltd.
11 Hellesdon Park Ind. Est.
Drayton Road, Norwich
Norfolk, NR6 5QR

Art - Effects
Unit 1A Moor Field Farm
Warkton, Kettering
Northants, NN16 9XJ

E Milner (Oxford) Ltd.
Canterbury Works,
Glanville Road, Oxford,
OX4 2DB

**Park End Antiques and
Interiors**
10 Park End Street
Oxford, OX1 1HH

Relics of Witney
35 Bridge Street, Witney
Oxon, OX8 6DA

S Sylvester
Wester Inches Farm House
Inverness, Highland
Scotland, IV1 2AA

Artstore
94 Queen Street
Glasgow, Scotland
G1 3AQ

Period House Shop
141 Corve Street, Ludlow
Shrops, SY8 2PG

Period House Shop
65 Wyle Cop, Shrewsbury
Shrops, SY1 1UX

Half a Sixpence
The Borough Mall,
Wedmore, Somerset
BS28 4EB

All About Art
31 Sheen Road, Richmond
Surrey, TW9 1AD

Art Room
191B High Street,
Guildford, Surrey
GU1 3AW

Brackendale Gallery
1 Sparvell Way, Camberley
Surrey, GU15 3SF

Caves Picture Shop
44/46 Church Street
Weybridge, Surrey
KT13 8DP

O W Annetts & Sons Ltd.
22A Upper High Street
Epsom, Surrey, KT17 4QJ

Wood Finish
30 The Vineyard
Richmond, Surrey
TW10 6AN

In-Perspective
58 George Street, Hastings
Sussex, TN34 3EE

Bryant and Goodall
Shop 3 Holliday Wharf
164 Holliday Street
Birmingham
W. Midlands, B1 1TJ

Gough Brothers
71A High Street
Bognor Regis, W. Sussex
PO2 11RZ

Welcome Home
18A Warwick Street
Worthing, W. Sussex
BN11 3DJ

Decorative Designs
Arwel, Moelfre, Anglesey
Wales, LL72 8HW

Neil Chambers
Trend of Worcester
14 Friar Street, Worcester
Worcs, WR1 2RZ

The Village Idiot
12 Hewell Road
Barnt Green, Worcs
B45 8NE

Screens & Co.
Cherry House, High Street
Whixley, Yorks, YO5 8AW

Acknowledgments

This book could not have been produced without the tremendous assistance of the Home Team – David, Henry, Felix, and Hugo – and the Away Team – Geoff "Lighting" Dann, a photographer with a keen sense of atmosphere in the studio and in his photographs, Gavin "Latino" Durrant, a photographer's assistant without parallel, and Steve "The Socks" Wooster, a designer with a great awareness of time and place. Many thanks also to Colin Ziegler, Claire Waite, and Gabrielle Townsend for their patience and understanding.

I am also very grateful to Eri Hz. Heiliggers who gave expert advice on woodgraining and provided the grained samples on page 76, the grained case on page 77, and the marbled case on page 90; and to Kate Pollard who assisted with the sponged table on page 26 and the colorwashed fireplace on page 30.

I used my own range of paints, pigments, and glazing medium throughout the book (see the list of suppliers on the previous page and above), but I would like to thank the following for providing other materials: Polyvine for the varnishes (Polyvine Ltd. Vine House, Rockhampton, Berkeley, Glos. Gl13 9DT); R G Willis for the fire surround (Wessex Products Ltd. Unit 16 Harris Road, Calne Business Centre, Calne, Wilts. SN11 9PT); Finesse of Oxford for the plasterwork plaques, cornices, fireplace, and brackets (Finesse Ltd. Unit 5, 7 Westway, Botley Oxford); and Sue Teichmann for the wastepaper bin.

Thanks also to Lewis Ward of Whistler Brushes, whose specialist brushes feature frequently throughout the book (Lewis Ward and Co., 128 Fortune Green Road, London, NW6), and all those at Relics of Witney, especially Bret Wiles, Chris Walker and Ray Russell.